PRAISE FOR PASTORAL PREACHING

Unlike so many books on preaching and shepherding, *Pastoral Preaching* is thoroughly biblical, rather than anecdotal. It is convincing, convicting, and encouraging all at the same time. This book should become *the* standard text on pastoral ministry and preaching.

Rick Kress

Kress Biblical Resources

"We live in a day in which there is a famine in the land for the biblical preaching of God's Word and shepherding of His people. *Pastoral Preaching* provides much needed food in this crisis. Richard Caldwell has done all expositors a great service by building a bridge between preaching and pastoring by showing the two as inseparably linked. This work should be welcomed by the seasoned pastor as well as those exploring a call into ministry. Thoroughly biblical, theological, and immensely practical, *Pastoral Preaching* is a must read for anyone serious about Paul's injunction to Timothy, "Preach the Word.""

Steven J. Lawson

President, OnePassion Ministries, Dallas, TX

I am grateful to God for Richard Caldwell's *Pastoral Preaching: Expository Preaching for Pastoral Work.* This book deals with two passions of mine–pastoral ministry and expository preaching–and Dr. Caldwell does a phenomenal job showing how these two disciplines interrelate. Every pastor who loves the Word of God, and the flock of God, will no doubt benefit from Dr. Caldwell's work.

Dr. Jason K. Allen

"In an age of domesticated pulpits and disheartened preachers, Richard Caldwell's excellent *Pastoral Preaching* gives us a catalytic vision of the sermon and the pastor. His essential point is dead-center-bull-seye: the pastoral office cannot be conceived without the work of preaching. As preacher, the pastor claims all things in Christ, surveys all things in Christ, and renews the heart, mind and soul in Christ. But none of this work is merely functional; it is shepherding work, soul work, such that flesh-and-blood people pass safely from the world of shadow into a world of love. The closing testimonies show just that, and remind us all of the power of the pulpit, and the church's great need of the day: pastor-theologians."

Owen Strachan

Associate Professor of Christian Theology, Midwestern Baptist Theological Seminary; Author (with Kevin Vanhoozer), *The Pastor as Public Theologian*

"PASTORAL PREACHING is a must read for the man who has responded to the high calling to lead the flock of God. Biblical preaching is empowered when the preacher proclaims God's Word as a shepherd. Richard Caldwell unwraps the essential relationship between preaching and pastoring in a compelling and persuasive manner. I was both blessed and challenged by this book and highly commend it."

Daniel L. Akin

President, Southeastern Baptist Theological Seminary

"Richard Caldwell's "*Pastoral Preaching: Expository Preaching for Pastoral Work* is one of the clearest books on the subject of pastoral preaching and expository preaching. He ably demonstrates how the two go hand in hand. Here is a well thought out theology and practice of preaching that will touch the lives of people where they live. I might quibble with the author over his understanding of the role of elders in the local church, but I'm deeply appreciative of his commitment to genuine exposition as pastoral care. Buy this one and read it!"

David L. Allen

Dean of the School of Preaching and formally Dean of the School of Theology, George W. Truett Chair of Ministry, Director of the Center for Expository Preaching, Southwestern Baptist Theological Seminary, Fort Worth, Texas.

Many wonderful volumes have been written over the years on the art, mechanics, and skill of Bible exposition. What sets Richard Caldwell's book apart is his commitment to shaping not only method, but also mindset. He calls the reader to carefully evaluate the salient biblical data on pastoral preaching, but he also takes the reader to a deeper level, examining the fundamental motivations that compel a man to preach. This book will challenge you to consider whether your preaching is self-driven or intended for Christ's sheep. If you are wondering what role your pastoral work plays in your weekly preaching, or if you are seeking to understand the dangers of a preaching ministry divorced from shepherding, you, and every seasoned shepherd-expositor, will benefit greatly from this work.

Jerry Wragg
Senior Pastor at Grace Immanuel Bible Church
Chairman of The Expositors Seminary

PASTORAL PREACHING:

EXPOSITORY PREACHING FOR PASTORAL WORK

Richard Caldwell

Pastoral Preaching:
Expository Preaching for Pastoral Work

© 2016 by Richard Caldwell
All rights reserved.

Published by Rainer Publishing
www.RainerPublishing.com

ISBN 978-0-9978861-6-0

Printed in the United States of America

To my precious wife Jacquelyn, my best friend and greatest encourager.
To all of my children and grandchildren – precious gifts from God.
To the church called Founders Baptist, the love of our life of ministry
and a congregation that we are blessed to serve and grow with.
To my fellow elders with whom I have the joy of sharing ministry.

ACKNOWLEDGEMENTS

I am thankful for the many people who read the manuscript for me and offered their feedback. A special thank you to my friend and fellow Master's Seminary cohort member, Dr. Paul Shirley. His feedback was tremendously helpful. I am thankful for my friend Dr. Jim Hamilton who read it and offered constructive criticism that helped sharpen and clarify some of my statements. I am thankful for Dr. Jerry Wragg who encouraged me on more than one occasion. I am thankful for Suzanne Wells who helped me edit portions of the work. I am especially thankful for the congregation that is Founders Baptist Church, and the faithful elders here. Without their support I could not have completed the project. Above all, I am thankful to God for my wife and family for the time they patiently allowed me as I worked. In the case of all of these that I mentioned (and any I overlooked), they are not responsible for any failures in this work. Those are mine alone. But they are responsible for adding great joy to my life, and for that I thank God through our Lord and Savior Jesus Christ.

CONTENTS

INTRODUCTION
A PASTORAL MINDSET FOR PREACHING

There is no shortage of papers, articles, or books on the subject of preaching. The number of contributions offered on the subject of pastoral work is equally impressive. Why, then, am I writing on *pastoral preaching*? My hope is that pastors would be convinced that preaching is a means for pastoral work (caring for the church in a personal way), and pastoral work is an application of preaching. In what follows I make the case that these two subjects (preaching and pastoral work) must be joined in our thinking.

Preaching is a Pastoral Work

In his introduction to Samuel Volbeda's, *The Pastoral Genius of Preaching*, Carl Kromminga observed, "that in the United States in the nineteenth century 'Pastoral Theology' was considered a catch-all theological classification containing approximately all the operational disciplines except Homiletics."[1]

It is my contention and concern that this dividing of Homiletics from Pastoral Theology has not ceased. God's Word calls for both preaching and pastoral work. Are these two responsibilities divorced from one another?

Can they be faithfully executed when such a divorce occurs? Can pastors care for the church effectively without a faithful preaching ministry at the center of church life? Can one rightly communicate the Word of God powerfully without the mindset and the aim of a shepherd?

Samuel Volbeda emphasized this point nearly a century ago.[2] He argued that the genius (i.e. the distinguishing characteristic) of preaching is that it is pastoral. He wrote, "It has reference to the sermon preached and to the person preaching it. It follows obviously that, if preaching be essentially a pastoral affair, not only the sermon must have a pastoral quality, but the *preacher* too must have a *pastoral spirit*; he must also be a *pastoral man*. Hirelings and strangers may conceivably go through the routine of shepherding a flock, but shepherds they are not; and time and tests will tell the story."[3]

Biblical preaching requires that preachers enter the pulpit as shepherds. The pastor is not simply a dispenser of information. He is not a professional orator attempting to impress the listener with his own cleverness and skill as a speaker. He is not a spiritual marketer who is trying to get his finger on the pulse of what would interest and attract the listener. The man who faithfully preaches is the man who loves God and His church, and therefore watches for souls. He should have the mindset and aim of one who is called by God to shepherd the church through the careful teaching and application of the Word of God. *Preaching* is a *pastoral* work.

Charles Jefferson wisely observed "When the minister goes into the pulpit he is the shepherd in the act of *feeding*, and if every minister had borne this in mind many a sermon would have been other than it has been. The curse of the pulpit is the superstition that a sermon is a work of art and not a piece of bread or meat... Sermons, rightly understood, are primarily forms of food. They are articles of diet. They are meals served by the minister for the sustenance of spiritual life. If this could be remembered it would help many a minister to get rid of his stilted language and to cut off a lot of his rhetorical ruffles; it would free him from his bombastic elocution and burn up his ornamental introductions and skyrocket perorations."[4]

Pastoral Work Requires Preaching

At the same time, the aspects of *biblical pastoral work* that are outside of preaching still require the faithful preaching ministry of the Word of God. No church can be loved and cared for properly when it is not being consistently washed by the careful and powerful preaching of Scripture. It is not, therefore, preaching *or* pastoral care. It is preaching that shepherds and shepherding that relies on preaching. My focus is on preaching as a pastoral work.[5]

What I am describing requires a big-picture vision of the ministry of preaching. It is a vision of *preaching* informed by a thoroughly biblical view of what it means to be a *pastor*. True shepherding happens when pastors embrace *all* that God has revealed about *all* of their work. A biblical view of *preaching* is the result of the conviction that God's Word is the inerrant, authoritative, and all-sufficient standard for *all of ministry*. If preaching is to be what God means for it to be, then preachers must embrace what God means for *them* to be. This happens as pastors embrace a biblical vision of the church, of their office, and of their God-given mandate. My sole concern, then, is not for a particular *method* for preaching; but a *mindset* for preaching.

Who Needs a New Mindset?

The need for a better understanding of pastoral preaching is not limited to a single segment of contemporary evangelicalism. Too often, those who place great emphasis on the importance of preaching immediately conclude that a subject like this one is not a concern for them. For those who are wholeheartedly committed to careful exegesis and biblical exposition, the first instinct is to identify preaching deficiencies with those who do not seem as concerned about such things. But it is possible to have the highest view of Scripture, and the highest view of the importance of preaching, and still fail to practice preaching as a pastoral work.

On the one hand, contemporary preaching often defines good preaching in the terms of relevance. The main concern is that the sermon *connects* with the listeners. Much contemporary preaching is designed entirely around the concept of speaking to people's felt needs. This *feels* like preaching with a pastor's heart. After all, if you are a pastor, should you not be concerned about "scratching the itch," answering the questions your people are asking?

On the other end of the preaching-style spectrum are those most concerned with the *content* of the sermon. The chief ambition is biblical accuracy through the careful work of systematic exegesis. This is not wrong; an orthodox bibliology requires nothing less. It must be admitted, however, that a mindset which views preaching completely in terms of information impartation has contributed to producing many a congregation that is heady but not healthy, informed but not transformed. John Piper perceptively described a different approach in his foreword to Jason Meyer's *Preaching: A Biblical Theology* when he wrote, "...the main aim of preaching is not the transfer of information, but an encounter with the living God. The people of God meet God in the anointed heralding of

God's message in a way that cannot be duplicated by any other means. Preaching in a worship service is not a lecture in a classroom. It is the echo of, and the exultation over, God speaking to us in his word."[6]

Many pastors view their preaching ministry in one of two ways: preaching that is either aimed at the congregation's heart (emotions) or aimed at the congregation's mind (intellect). The biblical paradigm for ministry embraces a view of preaching that proclaims and applies the whole counsel of God's Word, which addresses the whole of man's nature, in order to accomplish the whole of what God has revealed as the standard of caring for His people. Such a view represents the compass for faithfulness in pastoral preaching.

Pastoral Preaching Mediates the Care of the Chief Shepherd

What many fail to fully appreciate is that the pastor is shepherding someone else's flock (Christ's). The pastor doesn't know the flock the way the Chief Shepherd does, nor is the pastor qualified to know best what meets the needs of that flock. What is often forgotten by those obsessed with relevance is that the pastor is a steward. He has not only been given a stewardship when it comes to the people he shepherds, he has also been given a stewardship of the message the Chief Shepherd has provided for their spiritual food. His task is not to invent what feeds them; he is to proclaim faithfully what God has supplied for their nourishment. As John Stott noted when discussing the pastor as a steward, "Indeed, if the metaphor teaches anything, it teaches that the preacher does not supply his own message; he is supplied with it."[7]

That is not to say (as I will explore later) that the pastor is not to be sensitive to the needs of people in his selection of the biblical material to be proclaimed at any given time. Nor is it to deny that the pastor's knowledge of his people is appropriately involved in the preparation of sermons. Rather, it is to insist that God has given *the Bible* for both the pastor's soul and theirs.

There are four main sections that make up this book and chapter divisions that make up those sections. The four main sections concentrate on the *biblical mandate for pastoral preaching*, the *elements for pastoral preaching*, the *motivation for pastoral preaching*, and the *method for pastoral preaching*. The chapters found in each of those sections will concentrate on specific matters that pertain to those big-picture items. Some of what I will discuss will be basic to preaching in general. Even so, the pastoral mindset that I'm arguing for is vital for the proper practice of any and all of the basic matters that relate to preaching. I trust that if the reader will consider each chapter with the overall thrust of the work in mind, how these various issues relate to one another will become clear.

At the end of the book is an appendix of personal testimonies from believers who share their stories of how pastoral exposition has served to shepherd them through some difficult circumstances. They serve to demonstrate that what we are considering in this book is not theoretical, it is all very real, and it is vital.

Our day is a day of great need but also a day of great potential and opportunity. The need of the day, specifically the need of the church, is pastoral work through expository preaching.

PART ONE
THE MANDATE FOR PASTORAL PREACHING

CHAPTER ONE
NEW TESTAMENT EVIDENCE FOR THE MANDATE

What I refer to as pastoral preaching is nothing new. In a day and age of novelty and marketing—selling what is cheap and common as though it were cutting edge and newly discovered—I'm arguing for something old. Rediscovery is the driving force for this book. The goal is for preachers who will have no other aim and no other motive than to preach in a way that represents what God meant for preaching to be. If one has forgotten, or never been taught, what preaching was meant to be, then may there be a rediscovery of the divine design. If one is already laboring to be a pastoral theologian, faithful to God's Word and to God's people, then may there be refreshment and reinforcement.

Pastoral preaching is expository preaching with a pastoral trajectory. It is expository preaching as the means for pastoral work. It is the preaching of the Word of God with the heart, and discernment, and aims of a shepherd. It is the practice of an understanding that the study of God's Word and the proclamation of God's Word is on behalf of the Chief Shepherd of the church, in the interest of feeding and caring for His people. Such a view of preaching, and such an approach to preaching, is mandatory. It is mandatory if God is to be obeyed and honored. It is mandatory if the preacher is to prove faithful to what God intends for preachers to be. And it is mandatory if the church is to be healthy.

While pastoral preaching is not new, there have been times in the history of redemption when it is scarce. It is my belief we are living in such a time. This scarcity exists on both ends of the philosophy of ministry spectrum. It is present where the content of preaching lacks depth and precision, in the name of "reaching people," and it exists where preaching is focused on imparting biblically precise information but lacks the heart and concern for fulfilling Christ's mandate to shepherd His sheep.

Preaching and Pastoral Work Connected

Literature abounds on the two subjects of preaching and pastoral ministry. However, my concern is to show how these two areas of God-given responsibility *require* each other. While a nod is often given by one of these areas of concern to the other, a concentrated emphasis on integrating the two is largely absent.[8] To put it simply, preaching and pastoral ministry are treated separately, compartmentalized as two completely distinct activities. Most would acknowledge both are biblical mandates. What is needed, however, is the *explanation and emphasis* that one must not be divorced from the other. Pastoral ministry must incorporate the work of the pulpit, and preaching must never abandon pastoral responsibility.

Pastoral responsibilities offer God-given opportunities for the reiteration and application of preaching. Preaching responsibilities offer a God-given opportunity and means by which one shepherds the church. Therefore, one must never be abandoned in the practice of the other.

Preaching and Conformity to Christ

The claim that preaching and pastoral work require each other is based on the character of Christ's relationship to His people as revealed in the Word of God. It is also based on the direct instruction Scripture gives for pastoring and preaching. Preaching is a work carried out in submission to the church's Lord.

Christ is the Head of the church (Eph 1:22; 4:15; 5:23; Col 1:18). He is the cornerstone of the church (Eph 2:20; 1 Pet 2:6; Acts 4:11). He is the Chief Shepherd of the church (1 Pet 5:4). He is the bridegroom of the church (Rev 19:7; 21:9; 22:17; Eph 5:25), and He is the owner of the church, having purchased the church by His own blood (Acts 20:28; 1 Pet 1:18-19; Rev 5:9). He is also the builder of the church (Matt 16:18). He is the gift-giver to the church, having supplied through the Holy Spirit every spiritual gift the church needs for its growth and spiritual health (Eph 4:8-16). He is the goal of the church. The goal for every believer is the maturity represented by Christ's own image (Eph 4:13). Furthermore, as the Chief Shepherd, He will one day judge and reward each one who stepped into the office of shepherd-teacher to His church (1 Pet 5:4; James 3:1). He has also given the commission that speaks of the ongoing mission of His church (Matt 28:19-20). Thus, the greatest urgency and highest priority in the work of preaching is to be faithful with respect to the character and purposes of Christ.[9]

Preaching is a Shepherd's Work

The biblical view of preaching is that it is a shepherd's work. The following evidence reveals that preaching is to be approached pastorally: (a) the New Testament charges given to the men who lead and teach the church; (b) the New Testament descriptions of those who teach the church and the context in which those descriptions are found; (c) the self-revelation of God that makes use of the shepherd analogy and manifests a concern for the instruction and care of His people; (d) the use of shepherding analogies in the Old and New Testaments to describe faithful preachers and to condemn unfaithful preachers.[10]

The biblical data points to a conclusion: preaching and pastoral care are not two tangentially related concerns, but two aspects of a single concern. Shepherding is the single concern. Shepherding is the overarching goal and preaching serves to that end and with that aim. Shepherding is the overarching goal because shepherding is the larger category within which preaching functions. Putting an arm around a grieving believer at a funeral, praying with a family as a loved one heads into surgery, counseling a couple struggling in their marriage, and meeting with a young man who is considering attending seminary are all examples of the work of shepherding and yet are not acts of preaching. But preaching to the church is *always* an act of shepherding. A pastoral trajectory for preaching is a sense of holy responsibility before God for the spiritual care of His sheep, and it is mandated by Scripture.

New Testament Evidence for the Necessity of Pastoral Preaching

Scripture often presents Christ as shepherd. He is anticipated in this way through the Old Testament prophets, and kings, and types (e.g. Ezek 37:16-28). He explains Himself making use of this metaphor (John 10:1-18). The New Testament writers describe Him in this way and His relationship to His church is often described in this way (cf. Heb 13:20; 1 Pet 2:25; John 10:25–30). Christ charges His disciples to care for His people as a shepherd. The Chief Shepherd entrusts the care of His people to under-shepherds who faithfully represent His will and desires. Those who serve under this Chief Shepherd in the work of caring for His people must manifest His mind, heart, and will, as they carry out His assignments. This includes the work of preaching.

New Testament Charges

Perhaps the most famous charge concerning pastoral ministry is found in Peter's encounter with the resurrected Christ (John 21:14-21). Following Peter's threefold denial of Christ, Jesus allows Peter three opportunities to affirm his love for his Lord. Three times Jesus charges Peter to care for His people and each time He does so using the shepherding analogy.

Christ's Charge in John 21

In this passage Jesus commands Peter to feed His lambs: βόσκε τὰ ἀρνία μου (John 21:15). [11] He commands Peter to shepherd His sheep: ποίμαινε τὰ πρόβατά μου (John 21:16). He then commands Peter to feed His sheep: βόσκε τὰ πρόβατά μου (John 21:17). In each instance Christ makes plain that He is ultimately in charge. The lambs and the sheep belong to Christ. Peter is to love Jesus by shepherding His people, and he is to do this by feeding them.

Twice Jesus uses an imperative form of a verb (βόσκω) that means to feed, to cause to graze, or in a more general sense, to tend.[12] It is used in the gospel accounts of pigs feeding (cf. Mat 8:30; Mark 5:11; Luke 8:32). It is used in reference to the prodigal son who was sent to feed pigs (Luke 15:15). This repeated commandment from Christ emphasizes the necessity of feeding Christ's sheep as an integral part of shepherding those sheep.

Robert Mounce, commenting on this passage, wrote, "Jesus' charge to Peter ('feed my lambs') underscores the basic responsibility of those who minister in the local church as pastors and teachers. Sadly, the business of the church and the felt needs of a congregation tend to usurp a pastor's time and energy. As a result, the flock goes hungry and problems multiply exponentially. Jesus has commissioned the clergy to be pastors, not livestock herders. The measure of ministers' love for Jesus is clearly demonstrated by their willingness to feed those entrusted to their care."[13]

John Calvin understood Jesus' command to feed in a more general sense, as imparting a responsibility to govern, but also noted the preaching responsibility necessary to such governance. Calvin said that Christ is the food for the souls of His sheep, and He uses men to preach that doctrine. He said that those men govern the church through the ministry of the Word, under Christ. Shepherding is the overarching concern and the ministry of the Word is a work necessary to that governance.[14]

I would also note that Calvin stressed the fact that the men called pastors take their name from the church's only true pastor. That is, he stressed what I emphasize when I say that Christ's own character and the purposes of Christ form the standard for the preacher. Preaching, in the final analysis, is about conformity to Christ, as is the whole Christian life. If Christ is our great shepherd then the work of the ministry, including preaching, must be the work of a shepherd.

Paul's Charge in Acts 20

A second important passage demonstrating that preaching and pastoral care are joined together is found in the book of Acts. The apostle Paul met with the Ephesian elders for the final time. In that meeting he exhorted them to be faithful shepherds to the church. He exhorted them, not only with direct words of instruction for their own work, but also by his own example that they knew well (Acts 20:17-27, 33-35). He charged them to be on guard for themselves and the flock (Act 20:28). He specifically reminded them it was the Holy Spirit of God who made them overseers, and the purpose for which He did so. They were made overseers to shepherd (ποιμαίνω) the church of God, which he obtained with his own blood (Acts 20:28).

Again, we find the same common elements that existed in Christ's charge to Peter. The church is not theirs but Christ's. They are given a responsibility for the church in the most serious terms. They are called to be spiritual guardians, and this is clearly analogous to a shepherd's work.

Paul then gave strong warnings. He was certain they would have to fight off spiritual wolves. The flock would be under attack from without and from within (Acts 20:29-30). Paul called upon them to be spiritually alert and to remember his tearful admonishments over the space of three years that were meant to prepare them for this responsibility (Acts 20:31).

But how were these men to keep watch for the souls of God's people? They were to shepherd through the ministry of the Word of God (vs.32). The dangers they would face would have to do with words, with false preaching and false doctrines. The danger, then and now, is in what the wolves speak (vs.30). The answer, then and now, will be God working through the Word of His grace. Paul left them to nothing more than God and His Word, and he was confident this would be sufficient for their task (vs.32).

Paul underscored the centrality of the Word of God in this work by noting what the Word of God's grace is able to accomplish. It is able to build up believers and to give them an inheritance among all those who are sanctified (vs.32). That is, the Word of God is able to accomplish what they need in this life and to lead them all the way into their everlasting inheritance. Paul's message could not have been clearer. These men were shepherds and their work is carried out by means of God's power and God's Word. This is the very same work they had seen Paul perform.

Even when Paul reminded them of his ways he did so in a way that stresses his faithfulness in preaching. He did not shrink from declaring anything profitable (vs.20). He taught them publicly and house to house (vs.20). He testified to both Jews and Greeks of repentance toward God and faith in Christ (vs.21). His goal, even in the face of certain suffering, was to finish his course and ministry. He described that ministry as one received from Christ (stewardship), and requiring that he *testify* to the gospel of the grace of God. (vs.24). The word translated *testify* (διαμαρτύρομαι) means "to make a solemn declaration about the truth of something."[15]

Even as he sadly expressed that this would be his last meeting with them, he did so in a way that emphasized the ministry of preaching. They are those among whom he has gone about *proclaiming* (κηρύσσω – to preach) the kingdom (vs.25). Further, he stresses how he has fulfilled his personal responsibility to them because he did not shrink from *declaring* to them the whole counsel of God (vs.27). In verses 20–27 he made reference to preaching or teaching no less than seven times.

These are shepherds. Their work is the same work they had seen in Paul. Paul's work and their work is a ministry of the Word. These are not two moderately related works (shepherding and the ministry of the Word), they are one and the same. They shepherd in their preaching, and the Word of God is the standard for all of their shepherding. Paul's own preaching ministry in their midst had fostered a closeness among these men. He had modeled a pastoral ministry of preaching.

Peter's Charge in 1 Peter 5

A third important passage is 1 Peter 5:1-4. Peter exhorts the elders among those who would receive this letter to "shepherd the flock of God that is among you (vs.2)." These elders are commanded to give a shepherd's care to God's flock. He exhorts them as a fellow elder, which would also remind them of his own example (vs.1). He exhorts them based upon his witness concerning the sufferings of Christ. He exhorts them as one who has a share in the glory to be revealed (vs.1).

It should be no surprise that Peter's charge to his fellow elders would echo the charge he had received from Jesus personally. Again, the same basic elements are present in this charge as exist in the two previous ones. There is a serious stewardship entrusted, and a particular way it is to be executed. They are to shepherd the flock that belongs to God, and they are responsible to God for how they do this. Peter gives them a series of contrasts by which they can measure their faithfulness: Not under compulsion, but willingly; not for shameful gain but eagerly; not as men who domineer a congregation but as men who serve as examples to the flock (vs.2-3). And all of this is done in view of the return of the Chief Shepherd who will reward them (vs.4).

But is there an emphasis on the Word of God in Peter's charge? The answer is supplied in two elements. One, Peter makes reference to his witness (vs.1). The word is μάρτυς. In each of its uses in the New Testament it does not speak of simply beholding something, but *attesting* to something. It speaks of one who gives testimony, or in the case of a divine message, of witnesses who bear a divine message.[16] Peter is saying that he is one who testifies concerning the sufferings of Christ. That language is a reference to his overall ministry as a witness and a preacher.

Two, it should also be said that Peter's self-description of *fellow elder* would mean he is not exhorting them to a work different than his own. While his emphasis in these verses is more on the mindset and the manner of shepherding than its means, they would have been aware of Peter's own example in terms of the means.

It is Peter who reminds them that the gospel was present when they were regenerated (1 Pet 1:23). It is Peter who declares that the Word of God abides forever, and that it was this Word that was preached to them (1 Pet 1:24-25). It is Peter who tells them how to prepare to receive the Word of God. He tells them what kind of longing they should have for that Word, and what the results will be when they receive the Word (1 Pet 2:1-2).

These New Testament charges make plain that the call to shepherd necessitates the faithful teaching and preaching of Scripture. Preaching, then, is a pastoral work. Genuine pastoral work always operates in a context where the Word of God is honored and taught.

New Testament Descriptions

The charges we have just examined are interesting in light of the New Testament descriptions of those who lead the church. The church's leaders are described (in terms of their office and work) as elders (πρεσβύτερος), overseers (ἐπίσκοπος), and shepherds (ποιμήν). These three terms each have reference to the one office we commonly refer to as pastor. When one examines the passages where these terms are used it becomes apparent they are used interchangeably to refer to the same men, doing the work of the same office.

In Titus 1:5 and 7, the men are referred to as *elders* in verse 5, and as an *overseer* in verse 7. In Acts 20:17 and 28 the men are called *elders* in verse 17, and *overseers* in verse 28, while their work is described as *shepherding* in that same verse (vs.28). In 1 Peter 5:1-2 they are called *elders*, and Peter charges them to *shepherd* God's flock while making clear that this requires exercising *oversight*.

The Work of Elders

The term most often used to describe these men, when the office is being considered, is the term elder.[17] But the analogy used most often to describe their work is that of the shepherd. The elders rule the church, but it becomes plain that they rule (oversee) as humble shepherd-leaders. This, the shepherding analogy, is the predominant one, and the one that sums up and encompasses what is included in the others. The elders shepherd. The overseers shepherd. The shepherds are to be spiritually mature men (elders) who watch for souls (oversee).

This is something crucial to understand because (as will later be explored more fully) Christ presents Himself as the shepherd of the church. His servants who serve as shepherds to the church do so by His appointment, and according to His instruction and example. He is described as the shepherd and overseer of our souls (1 Pet 2:25). It is interesting that at least three times in the book of Revelation, Christ is called shepherd in a context where ruling and guidance are prominent ideas. He *rules* (ποιμαίνω – to act as shepherd) the nations with a rod of iron (Rev 2:27). It is as shepherd to those who come out of the great tribulation that Christ *guides* them to springs of living water and wipes away every tear from their eyes (Rev 7:17). The vision of Christ striking down the nations with a sharp sword, and treading the winepress of the fury of the wrath of God almighty, is accompanied by the promise that He will rule (ποιμαίνω – act as shepherd) the nations with a rod of iron (Rev 19:15).

Christ's example teaches us to think of the shepherding analogy as the primary one, one that includes the need for spiritual maturity, and includes the work of ruling, guiding, or teaching. He is the perfectly wise shepherd who oversees our souls. His oversight is a shepherding work.

The Mindset for Elders

It is important to remember the primacy of the shepherd analogy because of its emphasis on strong, genuine, and sacrificial love. The Scriptures describe faithful spiritual shepherds has having a genuine, loyal, sacrificial, protective, and providing, care for the flock they lead. It is Jesus who described Himself as the good shepherd who lays down His life for His sheep. He is not a shepherd who runs when he sees the wolf coming (John 10:11-12). This is what the apostles of Christ saw in their Lord, and this is what they learned and taught when it came to the work of shepherding the church.

When we examine the attitudes expressed by the apostles toward the churches, and remember that they were the shepherds who taught and appointed the elders for those first churches, a picture emerges of what it means to shepherd the church. The shepherds of the church are called *overseers*. The example of those first shepherds teaches us that the oversight of the church is a work of love. It is not the cold business management of a corporate board, but the life or death struggle of spiritual fathers for their children. The shepherds of the church are called *elders*. The wisdom and maturity needed is because of the preciousness of the church to Christ. It is a weighty responsibility to shepherd the church, one requiring mature wisdom and experience. As the Ephesian elders were reminded, those who care for the church (ποιμαίνω - *shepherd*) are caring for what was purchased by Christ's own blood (Acts 20:28).

It is not surprising, then, to see on the pages of Scripture the apostles expressing their love and concern for the people of God in remarkable ways. It is clear that these men who learned shepherding from the Great Shepherd of the sheep learned that their lives were to be wrapped up in the spiritual health, safety, and well-being of the people of God.

Paul held the Philippians in his heart (Phil 1:7). He cared for the Thessalonians like a nursing mother tenderly cares for her children (1 Thess 2:6). He expressed a fierce disdain toward any false teacher who would lead the Galatians astray (Gal 5:12). He was as one in the anguish of childbirth until he saw Christ formed in those Galatian believers (Gal 4:19). His struggle was not only for those whom he knew well, but also for those whom he had not yet met personally in Colossae (Col 2:1-3). Paul's love for the Corinthians was especially remarkable. He was a spiritual father to them (1 Cor 4:15). He loved them even when his love was not reciprocated (2 Cor 6:12-13; 7:2). A careful reading of the two letters we have of Paul's correspondence with the Corinthians leaves us with the unmistakable picture of the love a parent has for children even when being mistreated by his children. Paul made plain that his burden for the churches was one that consumed him (2 Cor 11:28).

But Paul's love for the churches was not one unique to himself. This is the kind of love he looked for in those to whom he entrusted ministry responsibility. Paul sent Timothy to the Philippians because of the unique concern Timothy shared for their spiritual well-being (Phil 2:20). Epaphras taught the gospel to the Colossians and struggled mightily in prayer for their spiritual well-being and maturity (Col 1:7; 4:12). All of the churches of the Gentiles were to give thanks for servants like Prisca and Aquila who risked their lives for Paul (Rom 16:3-4). Epaphroditus risked his life for Paul, found himself near death, and yet was concerned for the church of Philippi due to their anxiety over his sickness (Phil 2:25-29). There are other examples that could be given, but the point is clear. Whether it is the Ephesian elders, or these servants whom Paul mentioned in his letters, those who are entrusted with the spiritual care of God's people must share the shepherd's heart for those people.

This same love was evidenced in the other apostles. John found no greater joy than to hear of his spiritual children walking in the truth (3 John 1:4). Peter expressed a lifetime commitment to reminding God's people of the truths that they needed to know (2 Pet 1:12-15).

The point is unmistakable. When one reads the New Testament descriptions of those who lead the church, we are right to understand the primacy of the shepherding descriptions. Elders, overseers, and stewards are shepherds. The shepherding work is infused in all other responsibilities and assumed in all other titles.

The Means for Shepherding

It is also vital that both pastors and church members see how each of those roles is inextricably tied to the ministry of God's Word. The wisdom and maturity of the elder is due to the wisdom and maturity imparted by God through the knowledge of and obedience to the Scriptures. This is what Paul emphasized with respect to the Ephesian elders. He is entrusting them to God and to the Word of His grace, because of the all-sufficient ability of that word (Acts 20:32). The overseer of souls is one guided and informed at every step by Scripture. This is why Timothy must watch himself and his instruction. By doing this, he will save both himself and his hearers (1 Tim 4:16). The stewardship of God's house is carried out at the same time that the stewardship of Scripture is faithfully executed.[18] Timothy's task required him to guard, by the Holy Spirit's power, the good deposit that had been entrusted to him (2 Tim 1:14).

John Stott wisely observed that the stewardship of God's house involves the stewardship of God's Word. He wrote, "The Christian ministry is a sacred stewardship. The presbyter-bishop was described by Paul as 'God's steward' (Tit. 1:7). Paul regarded himself and Apollos as 'stewards of the mysteries of God' (1 Cor. 4:1) and, although Paul was steward of a special 'mystery' which had been personally revealed to him, (Eph. 3:1-3, 7-9) this is not a designation for apostles only, since he applies it to Apollos as well as to himself, and Apollos was not an apostle like Paul. 'Steward' is a descriptive title for all who have the privilege of preaching God's Word, particularly in the ministry."[19]

In every way and at all times the men who lead the church are shepherds and the shepherd's work is one faithfully executed by means of the Word of God. This is why the shepherd's heart is often expressed *in the context* of the shepherd's work of the preaching and teaching of the Word of God. The elders who rule well are to be considered worthy of double honor, especially those who labor in preaching and teaching (1 Tim 5:17). The imparting of the gospel took place in the sphere of the imparting of one's life (1 Thess 2:8). When Paul envisions himself being poured out like a drink offering, it is upon the sacrifice and service of the *faith* of God's people (Phil 2:17). When he related to God's people as a father would to his children, it was in a way that involved exhorting them, encouraging them, and imploring them (1 Thess 2:11). That is, it was in the role of a teacher.

When one pays careful attention to the New Testament descriptions given to leaders of the church, it becomes apparent that the work of shepherding is included in every other responsibility of leadership. It also is apparent that the entirety of the leader's work is joined together with the ministry of the Word of God.

CHAPTER TWO
OLD TESTAMENT EVIDENCE FOR THE MANDATE

The New Testament charges given to pastors, and the New Testament descriptions of pastors, are in complete accord with Old Testament revelation. While the church and the nation of Israel are distinct, the shepherding heart of God toward His people is emphasized in both Testaments. It is not surprising that the work of ministry is the work of shepherding, and that the work of shepherding is a ministry of the Word. The God who gave the Word is Himself a shepherd and therefore His Word is pastoral. The leaders, and those called to preach to God's people, are called shepherds because they are chosen by God to mediate His own pastoral care for His flock.

The Self-Revelation of God as Shepherd

The New Testament pattern for mediated shepherding by means of the Word of God was anticipated in God's care for His people in the Old Testament. The first reference to God as shepherd comes from the mouth of Jacob. In blessing Joseph, he said that God had been his shepherd all of his life to that very day (Gen 48:15). Later, as he explained how God had defended Joseph, he referred to God as the Shepherd of Israel (Gen 49:24).

When Joshua was appointed as Moses' successor, it was in a context where Moses expressed the desire that the congregation of the Lord would not be as sheep without a shepherd (Num 27:17). The same principle of the mediated care of Israel's true shepherd, God Himself, stands behind every shepherding analogy applied to prophets, priests, or kings.[20] Those who are called to shepherd are called to shepherd *God's people.* The flock is God's, He is the true shepherd, and those who shepherd His people are His chosen representatives. This includes David (c.f., 2 Sam. 5:2; 1 Chr 11:2; Ps 78:70-72; Ezek 34:23; 37:24). God's love and care for His flock is expressed in His promises of shepherds for His people who will reflect His own heart (Jer 3:15; 23:4-6; 1 Sam 13:14).

The fact that God has used mediators, however, does not diminish the emphasis in Scripture on God as Shepherd. The Lord is seen as Shepherd in Psalm 23. In Psalm 77, the writer declares that it was God leading the flock by the hand of Moses and Aaron at the time of the Exodus (Ps 77:20). There are many other places where God is described as the Shepherd of Israel (c.f. Ps. 78:52; 79:13; 80:1; 95:7; 100:3; Is 40:11; 49;9-10; Ezek. 34:11-16, 31; Mic 2:12; 4:6-8).

The Arrival of God's Promised Shepherd

In the New Testament these Old Testament allusions and promises find their fulfillment in Jesus (cf. Ezek 34:23; Mic 5:2-4; Matt 2:6). He had compassion on the people who were like sheep without a shepherd (Mk 6:34). He was sent to the lost sheep of the house of Israel (Matt 15:24). His saving work is comparable to the man who leaves the ninety-nine sheep on the mountain to save the one that is lost (Matt 18:12-14). Indeed, as we read the descriptions of Jesus and we hear Him explain His own identity and significance, we recognize that He is the fulfillment of the Old Testament shepherd promises and patterns.[21]

The God of the Bible is the Shepherd of His people and, in Jesus, He has come to shepherd them personally. Jesus is not only the Good Shepherd (John 10:11–18) who knows His sheep and gives His life for the sheep, He is also carrying out a shepherding work during His entire redemptive mission. Matthew Montonini points out how Jesus utilizes shepherd imagery when speaking of His death, His resurrection, and His judgment of the nations. Montonini writes, "Jesus utilizes shepherd imagery to announce His death and resurrection to His disciples (Mark 14:27–31; see Zech 13:7), and to gather the nations for eschatological judgment (Matt 25:32). As shepherd, Jesus separates the sheep from the goats—the former receive mercy (the inheritance of God's kingdom [Matt 25:34]), the latter receive a curse (eternal fire [Matt 25:41])."[22]

The New Testament epistles describe Jesus as shepherd. He is the great shepherd of the sheep (Heb 13:20), the shepherd and guardian of the souls of His people (1 Pet 2:25), and the Chief Shepherd (1 Pet 5:4). The last shepherd references to Jesus are found in the book of Revelation, where the promise of Isaiah 49:10 is fulfilled by Christ (Rev 7:17).

The Shepherd Analogy and the Ministry of the Word

The pattern which has become apparent, namely, that God is the shepherd of His people, that He mediates this work of shepherding through chosen undershepherds, and that He does so through a ministry of His word, is confirmed when considering how the true leaders of the people are often distinguished from false ones in both the Old and New Testaments.

It should be noted that on many occasions the language of true or false shepherds is used in reference to the political rulers of Israel. However, it must be kept in mind that the ruling responsibility in the nation of Israel was one vitally joined to the Word of God. Further, the use of the shepherding metaphor was not confined to the Scriptures, or to the leaders of Israel. This was a common metaphor applied to rulers in the ancient Near East.[23] But this analogy took on a special significance among the Israelites because of their unique covenant relationship with Yahweh. To guide the people well was to guide them in the way of faithfulness to the covenant set forth in God's law (e.g. 1 Ki 2:1–4). A faithful ruler was one who led the people according to God's own heart, the true Shepherd of the people (Acts 13:22). So, false shepherds are not just false prophets, but false leaders of the people on every level. All of Israel's leaders had a responsibility to be faithful to God's Word.

Frequently false shepherds are described as devouring the people (c.f. Is 56:11; Jer 6:13; Ezek 34:2). They do not feed God's people as a shepherd, but instead feed themselves. Micah 3:1–3 pictures false shepherds feeding themselves. They "eat the flesh of my people, and flay their skin off them, and break their bones in pieces and chop them up like meat in a pot, like flesh in a cauldron (vs.3)." Verses 5-8 pronounce judgment against false prophets, contrasting Micah's ministry of faithfulness with their faithlessness. This is immediately followed, however, by judgments pronounced against the "heads of the house of Jacob, and rulers of the house of Israel (vs.9)." Those rulers include the heads, the priests, and the prophets (vs.11). Those dark days will not be the end of the story, however. The day is promised when the mountain of the house of the Lord will be established as the highest of the mountains and people and nations will flow to it (4:1). In those days the nations will come "that he may teach us his ways and that we may walk in his paths. For out of Zion shall go forth the law, and the word of the Lord from Jerusalem. He shall judge between many peoples, and shall decide for strong nations far away... (4:2–3)." The glorious day envisioned is one wherein the divine King of Israel will shepherd them by feeding them and ruling them. He will teach the word, and He will judge in perfect righteousness, which is to say, in perfect agreement with that word.

The contrast between true shepherds and false shepherds is a running theme throughout the Old and New Testaments. The metaphor is applied at every level of leadership, be they prophets, priests, heads, or kings. But irrespective of the level of leadership described, two truths remain constant. First, the ultimate shepherd is God Himself, and second, the standard for faithful shepherds is the word of that God.[24]

We have already seen the New Testament's treatment of faithful shepherds, including the charges and office descriptions regarding pastors, and the descriptions of Christ's ministry. In addition, we have seen warnings like that found in Jude where it is said of false teachers, "These are...shepherds feeding themselves (vs.12)." Christ warns His flock about false prophets with the words "who come to you in sheep's clothing but inwardly are ravenous wolves (Matt 7:15)." Most understand *sheep's clothing* as indicating *the appearance of a sheep*, but other Scriptural references suggest a connection to the clothing of a prophet. Hebrews 11:37 speaks of the suffering people of God wandering about clothed in sheepskins (μηλωτή). The same Greek word is used in the Septuagint to refer to Elijah's cloak (c.f. 1 Ki 19:13, 19; 2 Ki 2:8, 13–14). Perhaps what Jesus had in mind in His warnings about false prophets is a wolf in the dress of a spiritual shepherd. Either way, it is clear that when

Jesus is warning about false teachers He is using the imagery of a flock and a tremendous danger to that flock.

The pervasive use of this analogy to describe those who lead the people of God, with the Word of God, indicates the pastoral nature of spiritual leadership. God's use of a shepherding analogy to describe both good and evil prophets connects shepherding to the responsibility of teaching God's people the Scriptures.

Part One Conclusion

The mandate for pastoral preaching is a cumulative one. When one takes the entire picture we have just seen in God's Word, it is impossible to think that preaching would be anything other than pastoral in nature.

Pastoral work and preaching must not be separated. Pastoral work must always be the application of the Word of God that is preached in the fellowship of God's people. Preaching must always have as its aim and heart the faithful shepherding care of the flock that belongs to the Chief Shepherd.

In their book entitled *On Being a Pastor*, Derek Prime and Alistair Begg make this same connection between preaching and pastoring saying, "Shepherding and teaching should not be separated. Preaching and pastoral work help each other. Visiting enhances our preaching in that it helps us to appreciate how our fellow believers think, their problems, and their temptations. When we preach to those we know well, and whose situations we understand, we apply God's truth more relevantly, almost unconsciously – and probably the less consciously the better. Our visits and counseling have greater relevance too, because the members of the flock associate us with the Word they have heard taught and preached, and in one-to-one conversations we are able to apply that same Word more personally and in greater depth."[25]

I would simply add that preaching and pastoral work do not merely help each other, they are united. God has wed them in His Word, and what God has wed no one should divide. The next question to be considered is how a pastoral mindset functions in the matter of preaching.

PART TWO

THE ELEMENTS OF PASTORAL PREACHING

CHAPTER THREE
PASTORAL PREACHING COMMUNICATES WITH MEDIATED AUTHORITY

It can be helpful to take a broad principle and analyze its elements. Having considered the mandate for pastoral preaching, we now identify eight elements of pastoral preaching that must be convictional on the part of the preacher. The eight elements are authority and accountability (this chapter); adoration, awareness, and accuracy (chapter four); and finally, affection and adversity (chapter five).

When I refer to pastoral preaching, I am stressing a mindset for preaching. The following elements give a description to that mindset. They must be the basis for ongoing examination since no pastor has arrived at a place where growth in these areas is not needed. This is not meant to be an exhaustive list of what is present in pastoral preaching. Others would surely add something to the list or state some of these elements differently. It is, however, a list that strives to summarize the biblical teaching concerning what will characterize those who faithfully shepherd the flock of God. I have not attempted to organize these eight elements in a way that would represent any fixed order of priority. In truth, all must be present for the pastor to be faithful.

Authority and Pastoral Preaching

There can be little doubt that the shepherds of the church have a real authority in the life of the congregation. In the book of Hebrews, the people of God are called to remember their leaders, the ones who have *spoken the Word of God* to them. It is clear that the same men who lead the church (elders) are the men who preach and teach to the church. Those whom they lead are called to consider the result of their conduct and to imitate their faith (Heb 13:7).

Pastoral Authority is Real

It is instructive that the term "leaders" is used in verses 7, 17, and 24 of Hebrews 13 without any distinction in titles or any additional description. In other words, the instruction given here applies to present leaders as well as past ones. Later, in Hebrews 13:17, the church is called to *obey* their leaders and to *submit* to them. The reason given is twofold: the present work of these leaders, and their future accountability.

Those who have spoken the Word of God to them are those who watch over their souls. This is *what shepherds do*; they guard the flock and care for their needs. Those same leaders (who teach them) will have to give an account for their work, and the way they have been shepherds to God's people. This is what they *will have to do* in the future. That future judgment is a serious one. The fact they are teachers means an even stricter accountability than their brethren (Jas 3:1).

These statements describe a two-way authority operational in New Testament church life. There is real authority that has been given to those who lead and speak the Word of God to the church. They are not to be ignored, but heeded. It is not just their preaching but also *their manner of life* that is to be remembered. This is a great reminder of the fact that the church's preachers and teachers (elders) are shepherds. An under-shepherd has been called to communicate *instruction and guidance.* That guidance is one that reflects the pastor's own submission to that instruction. He is subject to the same words he teaches. Therefore, his life is a lesson in itself. He guides by his example as well as his exposition of Scripture. The result is that these men are to be followed. This submission is so important that it is said to be for the profit of those called upon to practice it (Heb 13:17). This authority has come from God.

Pastoral Authority is Mediated

At the same time, this authority is a *mediated* authority, and as such is to be exercised humbly and submissively. The work these men do is one that has been *assigned* to them, and one to be carried out as a servant (Mk 9:35). Their authority is exercised in submission to the ultimate shepherd who is the ultimate authority. The leaders are as subject to God and His Word as the people they care for. In fact, these undershepherds are fellow members of the flock. They are sheep too. There is a mutual submission that exists among every member of the body of Christ (Eph 5:21). This is why the leaders are subject to church discipline like any other member of the flock (1 Tim 5:19-20). The attitude of these leaders is paramount. Their attitude must reflect this mediated role. The authority they have been given is for building up the church not tearing it down (2 Cor 13:10).

Pastoral Authority Understood for Preaching

What does this mean for preaching? Pastoral preaching reflects this authority in each of the ways I have just described. It is a real authority but one that is humble and submissive. It is a mediated authority. There is a sense of boldness, urgency, and finality present in pastoral preaching. This kind of authority is not located in the speaker but in the Scriptures. Hebrews 13:7 makes it clear that it is the mediated authority that comes from the Word of God they proclaim.

It is Confined to Scripture

The shepherd's rod and crook is the Bible. The only legitimate authority wielded by a pastor is that authority which is derived from Scripture, accurately conveys Scripture, and is completely submissive to Scripture. The fact that preaching is a stewardship allows it to be authoritative and humble at the same time. The authority of the pastor's preaching is dependent upon the submission of his life and message to God and His Word.

It is necessary to remember that the pastoral qualifications include the statement that an overseer is not to be self-willed (Titus 1:7). The word translated *self-willed* in the NASB, and *arrogant* in the ESV, is αὐθάδης and it means that this man is his own authority, that he is stubborn, and that smacks of arrogance.[26] MacArthur commented on this qualification when describing a pastor's character. He writes, "The term used in the Greek text is particularly strong. It means the *opposite* of having a self-loving arrogance, of being consumed with yourself, seeking your own way, satisfaction, and gratification to the point of disregarding others. A pastor should not be a person who could be called headstrong or stubborn."[27]

Certainly it is true to say that this should be his character when dealing with other people. It is, however, instructive that it follows immediately after Paul said that an overseer must be above reproach *as God's steward*. Taking these two things together is helpful. The preacher is God's steward. This means he is someone who is responsible to manage what God entrusts to him—in the way *God wants*. This will not be the consistent and faithful practice of someone who is characterized by doing his own will. This is true of preaching, and every other shepherding work that accompanies preaching. The faithful man is a humble and submissive man.

In a helpful book, *The Preacher's Portrait*, Stott examined five key New Testament metaphors for the preacher. He considered the preacher as steward, herald, witness, father, and servant. Each of these, in its own way, intersects with the subject of authority and submission. But the connection between authority, submission, and the concept of stewardship is especially striking.[28]

It is Explained by Stewardship

Before surveying the biblical references to stewards, Stott offered the following observation, "The concept of the household steward was more familiar to the ancient world than the modern. Nowadays, Christian people associate the word 'stewardship' with campaigns to raise money, and in our everyday vocabulary a 'steward' belongs only to ocean-going liners and big residential institutions. But in Bible times every well-to-do householder had a steward to manage his household affairs, his property, his farm or vineyard, his accounts and his slaves."[29]

It is that management of another's property and affairs that makes the New Testament comparison to the work of the ministry so instructive.

Both concepts (submission and authority) are included in the stewardship metaphor. To manage another's affairs and property speaks of submission; these things are the owner's, not the steward's. Yet it also speaks of authority, for in whatever way the steward is meant to manage these things, the owner has granted the authority to fulfill that management.

After surveying several examples of household stewards from the Old Testament, Stott observed, "From this it is evident that the steward was a man of authority in the household, exercising a fatherly supervision over its members, and that the symbol of his office was a key, no doubt to the store."[30] Stott goes on to demonstrate specific ways in which the authority of a steward was exercised in biblical times.[31] His summary of the data and its application to preaching is important for us to hear. He writes, "The stewardship metaphor teaches us the nature of the preacher's authority. The preacher does have a certain authority. We should not be afraid or ashamed of it. It is an indirect authority. It is not direct like that of the prophets, nor like that of the apostles, who issued commands and expected obedience...but it is still the authority of God. It is also true that the preacher who declares the Word with authority is under that Word and must submit to its authority himself. Here, then, is the preacher's authority. It depends on the closeness of his adherence to the text he is handling, that is, on the accuracy with which he has understood it and on the forcefulness with which it has spoken to his own soul."[32]

Notice that when Stott applies the stewardship metaphor to the work of preaching he makes mention of both the biblical text and the one who declares it. The text has authority that is all its own. It is an authority that exists if the particular preacher who declares it had never existed. Yet when it comes to the matter of preaching, the authority of that declared text can only be properly communicated when the one declaring it has himself come under the power of it. His humility and submission does not nullify the authority of preaching; it magnifies the authority of God expressed through preaching.

It is Illustrated by Christ

The character necessary for faithful stewardship was on full display in Christ's earthly ministry. The Chief Shepherd is the perfect model of an authority expressed through submission. Though He is God in human flesh, He carried out His ministry in complete submission to the Father. He came to do, not His own will, but the will of Him who sent Him (John 4:34; 5:30; 6:38; Heb 10 7-9). Christ's life and words were so perfectly faithful to the Scriptures that if one did not believe Moses he would not believe the words of Christ (John 5:47). Christ continually appealed to the fact that He spoke the Father's words—that He was giving the people the message He had been given. When one studies what Jesus said about this it is stunning. Again and again, though He was (and is) God in human flesh, He made an appeal that people hear Him because He was faithfully speaking a message that had been *given* to Him (John 3:34, 7:16, 8:26–28, 40, 12:49–50, 14:24, 15:15, 17:8).

It is Conveyed by Humility

It is the very fact that the preacher is a steward that imparts a sense of *authority* to his ministry. He has not come to do his own will, but to do God's will. He has not come to deliver his own thoughts, but to faithfully and accurately convey God's thoughts by giving God's Word, the Bible. The sense of certainty and authority found in his preaching is explained by the authority and absolute truthfulness of the message itself. He delivers that message with the boldness that reflects he is faithfully and carefully mediating a stewardship entrusted to him. He is a herald who delivers someone else's message (God's), and that message *must* be heard and believed.

But his preaching is also circumspect and humble. Unlike Jesus, the undershepherd is not infallible. He is in a place of great dependence in his role as herald. God must strengthen him if he is to faithfully execute his office (2 Tim 4:17). This does not mean, however, that he gives an uncertain sound. Rather, knowing God's truth is never uncertain, he studies to show himself a faithful workman with respect to God's Word (2 Tim 2:15). To the same degree he rightly understands the message, and does not deviate from that message, his words will carry the very authority of the one who gave the message to be delivered (Titus 2:15). The message itself is worthy to be heralded in a way that boldly insists it be heard (Eph 6:19-20). This, of course, is based on the conviction that Scripture is God's Word. It is based on the conviction that Scripture is an objective witness that is inerrant, infallible, sufficient, and complete. It is also based on the conviction that by God's grace, and the ministry of God's Spirit, Scripture can be understood; the truth can be known. If Scripture cannot be rightly understood, then the biblical exhortation to rightly handle the word of truth would be meaningless (2 Tim 2:15).

When someone departs from that view of Scripture, preaching has no authority. It is ironic when someone like Fred Craddock can recognize a problem in preaching, having to do with the matter of authority, and not recognize what is at the heart of that problem. In seeking to diagnose what he called "the pulpit in the shadows" (the declining influence of preaching) he gave the following as one of its causes, "[A cause] of the current sag in the pulpit is the loss of certainty and the increase of tentativeness on the part of the preacher. Rarely, if ever, in the history of the church have so many firm periods slumped into commas and so many triumphant exclamation points curled into question marks. Those who speak with strong conviction on a topic are suspected of the heresy of premature finality. Permanent temples are to be abandoned as houses of idolatry; the true people of God are in tents again."[33]

It is Possible Because of the Perspicuity of Scripture

Craddock recognizes that people long for certainty and yet advocates a model for preaching that is robbed of it. He recommends what he calls *inductive preaching*, by which he means (in my view) suggestive preaching. Rather than stand as a herald and declare the authoritative message of the King, the preacher is reduced to someone suggesting what he believes he hears from God through Scripture. He then strives to suggest to others that perhaps they should hear the same. Or, he proclaims his message suggestively and then asks them what they heard from God while he declared it. The preacher does not preach as one conveying a message that has authority, but as the title of his book suggests, As One Without Authority.

It is not surprising the pulpit would lose the ring of certainty when the preacher is not convinced there is an ascertainable and authoritative message that is objective to himself and his listeners. Such an approach is often couched in the terms of humility. In reality, at the heart of a view like Craddock's is doubt about the Bible as an objective standard of authority. Coupled with this doubt concerning the nature and function of Scripture, is the equal doubt concerning the perspicuity of Scripture. In what amounts to a double-blow against authority in preaching, Craddock says, in effect, "I am not sure that the Bible, apart from a listener, represents an authoritative word. But even if it did, I do not believe we can confidently assert that we know what that word is." When arguing for *inductive preaching*, he questions what constitutes an authoritative word. He writes, "It is not a matter of saying truth is subjective, but it is a matter of asking whether there is truth inseparable from its appropriation. Whatever may be a person's theology of the Word as Truth complete and valid and final apart from all human grasp of it, the fact is, the person cannot employ such theology as a working principle for preaching. If he does, he will either identify his sermons with that Truth, and the messianism implicit in that identification will show itself in many alienating forms, or he will be reduced to silence out of fear of distorting or reducing the package of Truth before him."[34]

Craddock argues that even if one holds that the Bible represents an authoritative word that exists outside of the experience of the preacher or listener, he still cannot proclaim it as a herald. If this is attempted, he will either equate his sermons with the word itself or be so fearful of getting it wrong that he cannot really proclaim it.

Such a view is nonsense. What he argues is that even if one were to agree that Scripture is an objective and authoritative word from God, one can never be certain a passage of Scripture is rightly understood. He further argues that if one believes that such certainty is possible then that person's sermons are being equated with Scripture.

He goes on to betray his own theology of the Word when he writes, "The fundamental error in this whole approach is the artificiality of the objective-subjective way of thinking. If the biblical text or the Word of God is objective and the human hearer is subjective, obviously the human is secondary, for the Word is the Word even if spoken into an empty room or into the wind. But that is a contradiction of what a word is. Whether one views word as call (Buber), event (Heidegger), or engagement (Sartre), at least two persons are essential to the transaction, and neither is secondary... It is in the sharing that the Word has its existence, and to catch it in flight in order to ascertain which part is of the speaker and which of the hearer is impossible nonsense."[35]

This is a great error. Craddock argues that Scripture is a means by which you receive the Word of Truth and that you only receive the Word of Truth when it *becomes* the Word *to you.* I have offered Craddock as just one example. He is by no means alone. When one does not have a proper view of the Scriptures, and a proper view of a preacher's role as a steward and an undershepherd, preaching is robbed of its proper authority.

Craddock presents a false dilemma. Contrary to what he asserts, one can believe in the objective authority of Scripture, the perspicuity of Scripture, and the responsibility to herald Scripture, and not act as a Messiah. Humility is not proclaiming Scripture as if it has no authority apart from the one who receives it. Humility is making plain to the flock that you understand and you want them to understand that a sermon only has authority to the degree that its interpretation of Scripture is sound. Humility embraces the responsibility to practice sound principles of interpretation in the work of preaching and to teach the flock how to do the same. When this has been done, and the sermon has faithfully communicated the biblical message, it is to be received for what it is, the Word of God (1 Thess 2:13). It is, then, the preacher's task to provide green pasture for the flock by expositing the Scriptures in a way that not only proclaims the truth with authority, but demonstrates how he has arrived at his understanding of what he proclaims.

Accountability and Pastoral Preaching

The responsibility of serving as a shepherd to Christ's flock is a weighty one. With the authority that is granted to the elders of the church come the warning and the promise of future review by Christ Himself. When Hebrews 13:17 calls for the church to submit to the elders it does so with the promise that elders will have to give an account to God. Peter exhorted his fellow elders to shepherd the flock of God and to do so in an appropriate way. He did this with the reminder that the Chief Shepherd will appear with His reward (1 Pet 5:3-4). James warned that those who teach the church (and he included himself in that number) will be judged with greater strictness (Jas 3:1). Paul compared his ministry to that of a master builder and described a time when his work, and the work of others, would be subject to examination (1 Cor 3:5-15). The many sobering charges given to men like Timothy evidence the accountability that belongs to the shepherd-teacher (1 Tim 5:21, 6:13; 2 Tim 4:1-2).

Accountable to God

The undershepherd is accountable for *souls*. The weightiness of his accountability is not just explained by the gravity of the knowledge that God examines him, but also the gravity of what is at stake. He has been called to account for the souls of men and women. This is not an ultimate accountability. Men and women make choices with respect to their own eternal well-being or ruin. But with respect to those responsibilities imparted by Christ to those who lead His church (to pray, to guide, to correct, to comfort, to warn, to protect, to be examples, and to teach), the man of God must strive to be faithful. The goal is to be able to say, with Paul, that one is innocent of the blood of all (Acts 20:26). There is no weightier calling than this.

Accountable Before the Church

Not only does the Bible bear witness of a present and future accountability before Christ, but also to a present accountability before the church. An elder serves in a public role. He is set by God before the eyes of the congregation as an example to the flock (Heb 13:7). As a result of serving in such a public way, he is subject to public accusation and ridicule that may not always be just. Because of this, the church is to be careful that no accusation is received against an elder without the requisite process of two or three witnesses. If, however, that elder has been found guilty of unrepentant sin, he is to be rebuked in a public fashion as an example for the rest of the church (1 Tim 5:19-20). This is not teaching that elders serve under the authority of the church in the fulfilling of their duties *as elders*. Rather, it teaches that all *members* of the church are subject to the discipline of Scripture, including the elders. It is a reminder (as was mentioned in the section on authority) that the undershepherd is *under authority* even as he serves *with authority* on behalf of Christ. In the same way, those who shepherd the church are accountable to one another. Paul's public rebuke of Peter (he mentions that Barnabas was led astray as well) at Antioch, demonstrates the kind of mutual accountability that exists among those appointed by Christ for the care of His church (Gal 2:11-14).

Accountable for a Self-Watch

Such an accountability before God and man requires a most serious self-watch before one's own conscience and the Scriptures. Any failed pastor's dishonesty and hypocrisy before others has always been preceded by the silencing of his own conscience before God and His Word. The venerable Charles Haddon Spurgeon emphasized the need for personal godliness in his *Lectures to my Students*. There he writes, "It will be in vain for me to stock my library, or organise societies, or project schemes, if I neglect the culture of myself; for books, and agencies, and systems, are only remotely the instruments of my holy calling; my own spirit, soul, and body, are my nearest machinery for sacred service; my spiritual faculties, and my inner life, are my battle axe and weapons of war."

M'Cheyne, writing to a ministerial friend, who was travelling with a view to perfecting himself in the German tongue, used language identical with our own: – "I know you will apply hard to German, but do not forget the culture of the inner man–I mean of the heart. How diligently the cavalry officer keeps his sabre clean and sharp; every stain he rubs off with the greatest care. Remember you are God's sword, his instrument–I trust, a chosen vessel unto him to bear his name. In great measure, according to the purity and perfection of the instrument, will be the success. It is not great talents God blesses so much as likeness to Jesus. A holy minister is an awful weapon in the hand of God."[36]

This is a major and often neglected emphasis in the New Testament. Paul told Timothy he must keep a close watch on himself. He uses a word (ἐπέχω) meaning (in that particular context) to fix his attention on, to pay close attention to.[37] Not only was Timothy to keep a close watch on himself, he was also to keep a close watch on his teaching. He was told this would result in salvation both for himself and those who listened to him (1 Tim 4:16). As Thomas D. Lea notes, when commenting on this passage, a leader's spiritual wandering leaves a congregation open to spiritual disease.[38]

Paul's exhortation to Timothy regarding self-watch was the rule not the exception. There are extended sections of Scripture where Timothy is called to guard himself (2 Tim 2:14–26; 1 Tim 6:9–16). This was also common in Paul's communications with other church leaders. Paul's instruction to the Ephesian elders was not just a call to pay careful atten-tion to the flock. He called the elders to pay careful attention (be on guard for) to themselves (Acts 20:28). Paul's concern for his own life included the self-discipline necessary to avoid being a castaway (1 Cor 9:27).

This concern for self-examination was not exclusive to Paul. When Peter exhorted his fellow elders he reminded them that they were to shep-herd God's flock willingly, not under compulsion, not for sordid gain, but with eagerness; not domineering the flock but serving as examples to the flock (1 Pet 5:2-3). Surely such an exhortation requires self-examination. The same can be said of the caution given by James that not many should become teachers because those who teach will be judged with greater strictness (Jas 3:1). Such a caution requires that the one who would lead the flock of God must pay careful attention to his speech.

Accountability Transforms Preaching

This sense of accountability, to God, to men, and before one's own conscience in the light of Scripture, will transform the work of preaching. The preacher's responsibility before God is the overarching one. Every other kind of accountability pales in comparison with this one, and is assessed in light of this one. Speaking in the sight of God is a constant theme in Paul's writings. He states clearly that if one strives to please men instead of God, he is no longer a servant of Christ (Gal 1:10). The apostles have been entrusted with the gospel and so they speak not as those who seek to please men but those who seek to please God, emphasizing that God examines their hearts (1 Thess 2:4). Those who faithfully preach the Word of God are not peddlers of the Word of God (καπηλεύω, those who would make trade of the Word of God), but men who are sincere. They speak as those commissioned by God, as those who speak in the sight of God in Christ (2 Cor 2:17).

This weighty sense of accountability before God for what one preaches is emphasized in 2 Timothy 4:1-2 where Paul charges Timothy. He solemnly charges Timothy to preach the Word by invoking the presence of God and Christ Jesus. He imparts this responsibility to Timothy while reminding him of Christ's future judgment. Such accountability is unmistakable in a passage like that one, but it is clearly implied in many other New Testament passages. As has already been demonstrated, the preacher is a steward of God's Word. A stewardship always involves accountability. This can be demonstrated from Daniel Wallace's observation regarding commands in the book of 2 Timothy. Wallace says, "By my count, there are twenty-seven explicit commands given in the body of this letter. In 27 words Paul tells pastors what to focus on. You have to be blind to miss the thrust of Paul's instructions here, because *eighteen* of those commands—fully *two-thirds*—have to do with the ministry of the Word."[39] When one takes to heart the fact of this kind of accountability before almighty God, for the ministry of preaching, it imparts seriousness and carefulness to the work of preaching.

The mutual accountability in the body of Christ (accountability before men) also informs preaching. The fact that discernment is to be practiced by the church (1 Thess 5:20–21), that not even an apostle is to be believed in a blanket way (Gal 1:8), that someone like Paul understood his own vulnerability (1 Cor 9:27), and that the Ephesian elders were warned that wolves would arise from their own number (Acts 20:30), is good reason for humility in preaching. As already noted, while preaching has authority, it is an authority that shines because of its careful knowledge of the weighty accountability that it carries. This horizontal accountability (among men) is also emphasized by the fact that pastoral qualifications are set before the church (1 Tim 3; Titus 1), that pastors are taught they must not domineer the flock (1 Pet 5:3), and that even when Timothy must insist on not being despised for his youthfulness, he is immediately instructed to prove himself by means of his exemplary life (1 Tim 4:12). Such passages remind the preacher that while he has the privilege of shepherding God's people, he is still a sheep himself. He is a member of the body of Christ. This attitude of humility must permeate his preaching even when reproofs and rebukes must be delivered (2 Tim 4:2).

What of preaching and the accountability that exists between the man and his own conscience? The writer of Hebrews asks the readers for prayer while noting that he has a clear conscience, and that his desire is to act honorably (Heb 13:18). This is an appeal to those who must hear him, and a way of confessing that his ministry to them is sincere. False teachers are described as liars whose consciences are seared (1 Tim 4:2). Paul calls Timothy to keep faith and a good conscience (1 Tim 1:19). He is warned that some have rejected this and made shipwreck of their faith. He specifically mentions Hymenaeus and Alexander as examples (1 Tim 1:20).

A. Duane Litfin observes how the strength of a good conscience goes hand in hand with a strong faith. He says, "These two always seem to travel together (cf. 1 Tim. 1:5; 3:9). Strength in the one is always combined with strength in the other. So also is failure in the one correlated with failure in the other. Thus **some** who **have rejected** (*apōtheō*, "a strong, deliberate thrusting away"; used elsewhere in the NT only in Acts 7:27; Rom. 11:1–2) a good conscience have also found **their faith** destroyed (cf. 1 Tim. 4:1; 6:10). Theological error is often rooted in moral failure."[40]

His observation that theological error is often rooted in moral failure is poignant. It is a sad reality, often witnessed throughout the history of the church, and often witnessed in our own day, that moral drift gives way to theological error (or vice versa). How many ministerial "stars" have fallen from the evangelical sky in our day? Many of these famous preachers seemed to shine so brightly, and for a time had national, or even global, influence. In many of these sad cases evidence of moral compromise was ignored, which gave way to theological concern, and then public disqualification.

We must not dismiss Paul's statement to Timothy that if one wants to be a vessel for honorable use, set apart as holy and useful to the master of the house, he must be a clean vessel (2 Tim 2:21). Such cleanness involves fleeing from sin and pursuing what is right with those who call on the Lord from a pure heart (2 Tim 2:19, 22). The Word of God is clear that the goal of preaching and teaching is the supernatural reality of transformed hearts and lives. Scripture teaches that the aim of the preacher's instruction is love that issues from a pure heart, a good conscience and a sincere faith (1 Tim 1:5). Such an outcome is not sincerely (or effectively) sought when the preacher himself does not keep a clear conscience and a sincere faith.

Even in this, the accountability existing between the man and his own conscience, a spirit of humility is to be manifest. Paul confessed that while he had a clear conscience, he was also fully aware of his limitations in the work of self-assessment (1 Cor 4:4). A clear conscience does not equal ministerial perfection. The one who examines each of us is the Lord. So, even while the preacher acknowledges the mutual accountability that exists in the church, and the importance of self-examination, he continually returns to his ultimate accountability before God.

CHAPTER FOUR
PASTORAL PREACHING CONNECTS WORSHIP AND PEOPLE

The ultimate priority for believers is the worship of God. Faithful pastors aim to preach in a way that connects the people of God to their highest priority and the ultimate reason for their existence. Through *adoration, awareness* and *accuracy* in preaching, the people of God are shepherded in the context of true worship.

Adoration and Pastoral Preaching

Pastoral preaching, at its heart, is an act of adoration. The preacher who understands his role as undershepherd always speaks on behalf of the Chief Shepherd of the church. If preaching is to be an act of worship, it requires the adoration of God on the part of the preacher, and it aims at the adoration of God on the part of the listener. Any approach to preaching, then, that would center on man instead of God, or turn preaching into a cold recitation of biblical facts, is ruled out. John Piper, in his preface to *The Supremacy of God in Preaching*, identifies the two parts to true worship and explains how they are united in preaching. He reminds, "There are always two parts to true worship. There is *seeing* God and there is *savoring* God. You can't separate these. You must see him to savor him. And if you don't savor him when you see him, you insult him. In true worship, there is always *understanding* with the mind and there is always *feeling* in the heart. Understanding must always be the foundation of feeling, or all we have is baseless emotionalism. But understanding of God that doesn't give rise to feeling for God becomes mere intellectualism and deadness. This is why the Bible continually calls us to think and consider and meditate, on the one hand, and to rejoice and fear and mourn and delight and hope and be glad, on the other hand. Both are essential for worship. The reason the Word of God takes the form of preaching in worship is that true preaching is the kind of speech that consistently unites these two aspects of worship, both in the way it is done and in the aims that it has."[41]

A right mindset for preaching is that of a worshiper. Submission to the authority of God, and sincere concern for one's accountability before God (our previous two thoughts), is the result of genuine devotion to God. The preacher is a worshiper, preaching to and on behalf of other worshipers, and always hoping to see, through conversion, the number of worshipers increased.

The one who preaches as a shepherd desires to teach God's people their highest priority and direct them there. The highest priority for the believer is the worship of God. When one preaches as an undershepherd he preaches to wed the hearts of his listeners to Christ. His mediated role is apparent in his aim. This is one of the distinguishing fruits when comparing a true teacher of God's Word with a false one. True teachers direct the people of God to Christ. False teachers desire to win people to themselves (Gal 4:17). If preaching is not an act of worship, it is worthless.

The apostle Paul gave a striking example of this contrast in the book of

2 Corinthians. In that letter Paul engaged in a battle for the hearts of God's people. He expressed this battle in straightforward terms when he wrote, "We have spoken freely to you, Corinthians; our heart is wide open. You are not restricted by us, but you are restricted in your own affections. In return (I speak as to children) widen your hearts also" (2Co 6:11–13).

For what purpose and to what end did Paul ask the Corinthians to open their hearts to him? The answer is that they had opened their hearts to false teachers, and Paul had to strive to recapture their affections to himself on behalf of Christ. In order to recapture their affections Paul engaged in what he hated. In the eleventh chapter he mounted a defense of his own ministry by contrasting it with the false teachers - teachers with whom the Corinthian believers had become enamored. In a different context it would have been utter foolishness (11:1), but Paul was forced to this defense (12:11). He used remarkable language that communicated several vital threads of concern that will be present in someone who shepherds and preaches with adoration for Christ.

For one, he communicated a genuine love for the people. He described his concern for them in the terms of godly jealousy (v.2). He was able to walk them through a list of his past actions toward them which had demonstrated the unselfish motives that characterized his ministry (v.5–10). He called upon God as a witness concerning his love for the Corinthian church (v.11).

Second, he communicated an urgent concern about their misguided loyalties. Paul clearly saw the false apostles as men who had wormed their way into the hearts of the Corinthian saints. These were men who proclaimed another Jesus, who represented another spirit, who presented another gospel, and yet the Corinthian church had opened their hearts to them (v.4). These false apostles boasted of their superiority in comparison with Paul, and they had slandered and mischaracterized Paul's motives and ministry. Paul could see that the Corinthians had been affected by it (v.5–10). Paul engaged in the defense of his ministry to undermine the deceitful claims of those false teachers. He wanted to make clear that they had not worked on the same terms as he did (v.12–13).

Third, Paul made plain that the Corinthian church was under assault by Satan. Paul's concern for the church was not selfishly motivated; it was spiritually motivated. He voiced his fear that just as the serpent had deceived Eve, so they were in the process of being led astray (v.3). The evidence of such deception was the acceptance of heterodoxy (v.4). The so-called ministry of the super-apostles was a great deception in complete accord with the one who disguises himself as an angle of light, namely, Satan (v.13–14).

Finally, and most importantly, each of these concerns was in the interest of something ultimately preeminent. Paul had betrothed these people. His love for them, and his desire for their love, was in the interest of a higher love, the love of Christ. His jealousy for them was a divine one, a godly one. It was jealousy for their single-hearted devotion to Jesus. His desire to reclaim their loyalties was not to win them to himself, but to Christ. His warnings concerning the deceptive nature of the false teachers, and the spiritual forces that stood behind that deception, were given so that the Corinthians would hold fast to Jesus. He had betrothed them to one husband, to present them as a pure virgin to Christ (v.2). He feared, lest by Satan's deceiving activity, they should be led astray from a sincere and pure devotion to Jesus (v.3).

At each point of Paul's concerns are the interests of His Lord. Paul worships and adores the Son of God. His relationship with the people of God is on behalf of a mutual adoration of Jesus. Remarkable and striking throughout such an example is the shepherding heart standing behind it.

It is the genuine shepherd who seeks to win his listeners to *Christ* precisely because of his love *for them*. True love for the people of God wants what is best for the people of God. It manifests itself by guiding them to true pasture. The Shepherd of their souls (Christ) is also the sustenance for their souls. They can only feed on Christ if their focus is on Christ. This directing of God's people to their Shepherd is a joyful task, not a reluctant one, when the one preaching adores the Lord Jesus Christ. It must never be lost on us that Christ's threefold charge to Peter (that he should shepherd the flock) was each time introduced by a question concerning Peter's love for Christ (John 21:15-17). Forever joined together in that encounter is the matter of adoration and the feeding of the flock.

This particular distinguishing mark of pastoral preaching (adoration) saturates the New Testament. One clear proof that adoration permeated the preaching given to the church is the presence of doxology in the New Testament. Doxology can be defined as "a short, spontaneous ascription of praise to God."[42] There are many examples of doxology in the New Testament.[43]

The presence of these doxologies demonstrates that worship is the atmosphere for instructing the church. Or, to put it more simply, the instruction of the church is an act of worship. The preacher not only instructs the church by means of words, but also by means of personal worship. As was noted earlier, it is apparent in the New Testament record that this love for God, this exclusive worship of God, was on display in the guarding of souls. It is pastoral ministry that guards the singular devotion of God's people. It is a true undershepherd who is fiercely interested that God's people not be moved away from their devotion to the Chief Shepherd. John the Baptist embodied a true messenger of Christ with his words, "He must increase but I must decrease (John 3:30)."

Awareness and Pastoral Preaching

Another element present in pastoral preaching is a shepherd's awareness of the condition of his flock and of the unique environment in which that flock currently exists. Preachers who faithfully shepherd the flock will see the need for a systematic and well-rounded diet for the sheep. The preacher's task is to proclaim the whole counsel of God (Acts 20:20, 27). He does this sensitive to the condition of the flock, and the promptings of the Holy Spirit. He does not approach his work of feeding the flock in a mechanical fashion, and his preaching reflects awareness of the specific challenges facing that particular body of believers. His task is to faithfully and systematically teach them the Bible in its fullness, yet in a way that shepherds them in the moment. He is not one who selects his preaching material from week to week based on his feelings. He is one, however, who knows how to depart from his patterned way of instructing the flock when the need arises, or how to fit that patterned instruction to the moment without doing violence in the work interpretation. In other words, with full confidence in the sufficiency of Scripture, and with the knowledge that all human beings have the same needs and temptations, he still preaches to the people sitting in front of him.

It is instructive to observe how often the New Testament letters reflect specific matters of concern facing the individual congregations, as opposed to a mere general and systematic instruction of the church. Even when the instruction is more general in nature, often there are evidences that the instruction is shaped, in one way or another, by the specific situation facing the recipients. I find it highly significant that God did not give us a New Testament consisting of generic teaching devoid of context specific details. Rather, in both Testaments, the timeless truths of the Word of God are communicated to God's people in a way that acknowledges the real life situations facing the original recipients.

For example, Galatians was shaped by the presence of a Judaizing influence and the danger of believers departing from the true gospel. Both letters to the Corinthians reflect a strained relationship that existed between Paul and that congregation. They also reflect specific areas of disobedience or misunderstanding in that particular group of believers. The letters to the Thessalonians reflect eschatological concerns and misunderstanding, and the spiritual instability that resulted. In the Pastoral Epistles, though the instruction is timeless and for all contexts, one can still discern specific challenges that faced Timothy and Titus in the cities and churches where they served. The book of Philemon arose out of a specific and personal interest Paul took in the converted slave named Onesimus. The book of James addressed dispersed Jewish believers in great need of encouragement and perspective in view of the distresses they faced. Indeed, each and every New Testament book, including the Gospel accounts, is recognized to contain something, or to be shaped by something, that pertained to its first audience. Looking beyond the overall theme of the New Testament books, and taking note of the instruction present in those books, one cannot miss the pastoral sensitivity present in the instruction.

The book of Hebrews is a particularly striking example of this. It contains some of the loftiest Christology found anywhere in the New Testament. That robust teaching about Christ, however, arose out of a pastoral concern. The writer of Hebrews argued for the perseverance of professing Jewish Christians who were tempted to apostatize. They were in danger of returning to Old Covenant practices and rejecting the New Covenant truth found in the Lord Jesus Christ. The theology the writer taught was in the interest of their perseverance and preservation. An analysis of the first chapter is enough to serve as an example of pastoral awareness and how it operates in preaching. I say "how it operates in preaching" because many scholars would agree that the book of Hebrews has a sermonic quality about it.[44]

This theologically rich sermon is driven by pastoral awareness. The book of Hebrews is full of warning passages. It is clear that the writer's concern was the potential spiritual defection of those who would hear his letter. So, how did he address their temptation to defect? His answer for their temptation was to set Christ's glorious person and offices before their spiritual eyes.

The writer of Hebrews declared the preeminence of Jesus in a sevenfold way in the first four verses. Christ was presented as the heir of all things, the one through whom all things were created, the radiance of God's glory, the exact imprint of God's nature, the sustainer of the universe, the one who made purification of sins, and one who is now seated at the right hand of the majesty on high (Heb 1:1–4). Following that sevenfold description of Christ's glorious person, the writer then gave seven Old Testament quotations that demonstrated what he has just declared in the first four verses (Heb 1:5–14). He selected passages emphasizing the Old Testament promise and expectation of Messiah as the greater son of David. He also selected passages that emphasized that this promised Son of David is also the Son of God, and the great high priest who atoned for the sins of His people. Taking passages meant to call to mind the overarching message of the Old Testament regarding Messiah, he made a theological and expositional case for the superiority of Jesus over the angels.[45] The writer did this to persuade those who would hear this letter that the covenant mediated by Jesus is better than the covenant mediated by angels. His point was that they must not turn back from Christ.

The letter to the Hebrews is a clear example that theological depth, careful biblical argumentation, and sober spiritual persuasion, can (and must) be present in sermons that are sensitive to the specific challenges facing a particular people at a particular time. The sensitivity on display is not just one of matching instruction to immediate needs, but also one of matching instruction to the spiritual condition and maturity of the recipients.[46] The writer of Hebrews noted the difficulty of instructing those who had become dull of hearing and ought to have been further along in their maturity (Heb 5:11-13). Paul told the Corinthian church that his instruction of them was restricted by their spiritual condition (1 Cor 3:1-3). Such sensitivity and wisdom reflects the example of the Chief Shepherd Himself (John 16:12). Pastoral preaching reflects that awareness. One important difference, however, is apparent. The authors of the New Testament were giving inspired teaching in answer to the specific contexts and situations reflected in their writings. Preachers today are called to take from the storehouse of that inspired revelation and communicate it to contemporary congregations with pastoral wisdom and skill.

Accuracy and Pastoral Preaching

The greatest need of the sheep, regardless of circumstances, and irrespective of their spiritual condition or maturity, is the need for the truth. The truth must be lovingly communicated based on the condition of the flock, but the truth is never sacrificed. Pastoral care in preaching requires biblical faithfulness in the pulpit. It never makes faithfulness to the text of Scripture a secondary matter for concern in the name of affection. To say it another way, one must never sacrifice carefulness with respect to the content of one's preaching, in the name of caring for a congregation. A shepherd's heart (manifested in preaching) will be evidenced by a man striving, to the best of his ability, to preach the Word of God with accuracy and clarity (2 Tim 2:15). George Knight, commenting on what the ESV translates as "rightly handling the word of truth," points out, "only when he handles it correctly will he be unashamed." [47]

Text Driven Sermons

To shepherd God's people well, the preacher must be convinced of the insufficiency of his own wisdom and the all-sufficiency of God's wisdom. That conviction drives the preacher to practice exegesis instead of eisegesis as he studies the Bible. The goal is to discover God's mind by reading "out of" the text of Scripture. What must be feared and avoided is reading one's own views "into" the text of Scripture.

Daniel Wallace sounded a much needed warning, addressing himself pointedly to the most learned, when he emphasized the need for a humble pursuit of God's truth. He wrote, "Quite frankly, the Church today is filled with workmen who have every reason to be ashamed. They have not grappled with the meaning of the text and hence they have not grappled with God's revealed will. They come to the Bible with their own prejudices and never adjust their life because they never see the truth. You might think that I'm not speaking to you. You say, 'I'm insulated from that error. After all, I know Greek and Hebrew.' In reality, those who know the biblical languages are in the greatest danger of abusing Scripture. Such knowledge is a profound trust. By the time you finish three years of Hebrew and Greek, you will know enough Greek and Hebrew to manipulate the text and justify your preconceived notions. And if you don't log *serious* time in God's Word, in a breathless pursuit of truth, submitting your life to what you learn before you speak to others, your congregation will pay the price, and it will be a very dear price indeed."[48]

Personally Encountered Sermons

Wallace mentions something absolutely necessary for accuracy in preaching. If the preacher is to rightly handle God's Word, he must come to that word submitting his life to it. The preacher comes to the Bible to be changed by God. He comes to the Word of God as a worshiper of God and a disciple of Jesus Christ. He does not come to get a sermon. He comes to have his own life transformed by the truth.

It is out of a personal encounter with the living Word of God that a faithful preacher delivers sermons to others. It is a heart that desires to know the truth that will strive to deliver the truth to others. Accuracy in preaching flows out of the spiritual integrity of the preacher. If his own faith is sincere, if truth is of utmost concern for his own life, then he will never settle for giving to others what he would not desire for himself. Preachers must heed Wallace's warning. We must handle the Bible in a way that is not shameful. "*That will preach*" must forever be jettisoned unless "*that is true*" can be said of the same material. Let any thought that pastoral preaching means more conversation with a congregation and less content, more tenderness but less truth, perish.

Accuracy in preaching is no easy task. While accuracy in preaching requires the sincere and personal desire to know the truth, it will also require more than sincerity. Greater is the number of preachers who call for accuracy in preaching than those willing to spend the time and effort necessary to accomplish it. Faithful preaching requires pastoral theologians. Before a man is an accurate preacher he is a careful and knowledgeable student. His carefulness is one driven by pastoral concern. A man preaching with a pastor's heart understands the need God's people have for the pure milk of the Word of God (1 Pet 2:2). He desires to see that need met and that desire drives him to carefully study Scripture.

Pastor Theologians

The church desperately needs a renewed vision of the pastor as theologian. Regrettably, some believe that the deep and careful study of Scripture takes place only in the academy. The assumption is that real study is found in the academy and caring for souls is found in the church. Accuracy is assigned to the realm of the professional scholar, while the caring application of such knowledge resides in the domain of the local church pastor. The thinking goes, "If one wants to learn theology let him sit at the feet of the seminary professor, the professional academician. If one wants to learn how to care for souls, let him consult the experienced pastor." If such a mindset is adopted, it is no wonder that local church pastors would care less about biblical accuracy than about the apparent comfort and help imparted by what they have to say.

Scott M. Manetsch produced a fascinating work on the pastoral theology and practical ministry approaches of the pastors who served Geneva's church during the years 1536–1609 (including John Calvin and Theodore Beza). In his research he found that *Calvin's Company of Pastors* provided the example of robust teaching coupled with exhaustive pastoral work.[49]

Pastors, in Geneva, were scholars and shepherds at the same time. Ministers were required to be engaged with the shepherding needs of the congregations, and were also expected to fulfill rigorous study require-ments. Manetsch writes, "The *Ecclesiastical Ordinances* (1541) mandated that Geneva's pastors be lifelong students of the sacred text; ministers who neglected their studies—and particularly the study of the Scriptures—were subject to consistorial admonition and even formal discipline."[50] Calvin and Beza made plain, however, that pastoral scholarship was always done in the service of the church.[51] For the emerging Reformed Church in Geneva, the pastor was a theologian whose scholarship served the church.

Today's pastors (and the church) should be grateful for godly scholars, and for every contribution made by professional scholars to the materials used to know the Bible better. But pastors should never accept the notion that theology is held captive by the academy.

John Frame, a seminary professor since 1968, argues passionately for a new model for pastoral training. He contends that the academic model for pastoral training has largely proven to be a failure. The church needs pastors that are both students of theology and skilled practitioners in its application to a flock. Theology, for Frame, always involves application. He defined theology as "the application of Scripture, by persons, to all areas of human life."[52] He emphasized, "If we define theology as teaching in this sense, then, we also know its goal, to bring spiritual health to its hearers."[53] Theology (defined as Frame does) is not content to live in the realm of the theoretical; it lives in the realm of practical devotion to God. And because theology is the application of the Word of God to all of life, it is a basic work that has been entrusted to the church. This work, accord-ing to Frame, includes the work of preparing pastors to do ministry who will then teach others to do ministry.[54]

Frame does not deny there is a place for traditional seminaries. Neither does he deny there is a need for professional biblical scholars.

But he rejects the thought that the work of theology is to be abandoned to the academy. There is more biblical warrant for local church pastors being the mouthpieces for theological transmission than there is for the academy being the vehicle for that transmission. Theology is transmitted through pastors by means of sound biblical exposition, and by the application of that exposition through pastoral work.

The Convictions that Fuel Accuracy

At the same time, it must be admitted that the academy has taken a larger role in the minds of many in our day because the pulpits of our churches have often proven anemic. The contemporary pulpit, in many cases, lacks the careful study of Scripture. If God's plan is for the church to be the pillar and support of the truth in this world (1 Tim 3:15), then pastors must repent of shoddy sermons devoid of content and indifferent to the Bible's rich theology. Topical preaching series that serve like how-to-manuals for hot-button issues do not represent the theological transmission entrusted to the church (2 Tim 2:2). Personal rants filled with the pastor's opinions and a selection of proof texts does not represent a pastor guarding the good deposit of the faith, a work for which the church is responsible (2 Tim 1:14). Accuracy in preaching is a matter of pastoral care and pastoral work. One cannot truly love the church of God (pastoral care) without putting forth the effort (pastoral work) to do one's best to discover what the truth of Scripture actually is, and to communicate that truth well.

Responsible to God for His Word

What will it require of us if we are to feed the people? Accuracy in preaching will require the right set of convictions. One strives for accuracy in the preaching of God's Word when he is absolutely convinced that he is responsible to God for what he says in the name of God. It is sinful to communicate ideas, commandments, permissions, or restrictions, to the people of God—in the name of God—that are not actually found in Scripture.

God Has Given What the People Need

Hand-in-hand with that conviction is the belief that what God has actually said is what people really need. A belief in the sufficiency of Scripture stands behind the conviction that one must handle the Bible accurately. The pastor must be convinced that his study time is a loving act toward the congregation he serves. He loves them as he works hard to rightly understand the text. He loves them as he prayerfully considers the best way to communicate that accurate understanding of the text to their hearts and minds. A well-taught church shares in these convictions. The more mature a congregation becomes the more that congregation appreciates the hard labor of sermon preparation. The pastoral preacher must be convinced that the call to love God, and to love God's people, is a call to rightly handle God's Word.

Faithfulness to the Text is Success

In addition, he must be convinced that preaching that is faithful to the text of Scripture constitutes success. It seems quite evident, and it is quite concerning, that many preachers measure the usefulness of a sermon, not by its faithfulness to Scripture (and therefore its accuracy), but by its apparent popularity with their hearers. If it is thought that success in preaching is measured by the response of listeners, a day will come when the preacher is not faithful to God. The Bible is clear there will be times when sound teaching is not popular (2 Tim 4:1–5). If the preacher adjusts his message in such times, in order to maintain favor with the people, he will prove unfaithful to God and to His word.

It must be stressed, however, that preaching which is faithful to the text of Scripture is not just a matter of information. Faithful preaching is preaching that accurately conveys the heart of God. I fear there are many who measure faithfulness in preaching by a wooden and mechanical standard. How sad it is when a preacher delivers the right words in an entirely wrong spirit. How often has a preacher delivered words of wonder with no sense of wonder in his words!

The Preacher Experiences the Text

This is why the preacher must come under the power of the text, in his own heart and life, before he can faithfully deliver it to others. He must be taught by God before he can teach God's Word. It is pastoral love that not only strives to get the message accurate but also carry that message to a people who are in the preacher's heart. Alex Montoya said, "A pulpit in the hands of an unbroken man becomes a throne from which he demands worship for his artistry. But to a broken man, the pulpit is a yoke that straps him to his fellow man to carry him along the road of life."[55] A preacher with a pastor's perspective works hard at how best to communicate the truth. He does this because it is the heart of God, and the heart of a pastor, that God's people would understand the truth. Faithful preaching is always striving to communicate the text in a way that would connect with the listener.

The point is, we must be clear on what constitutes faithfulness in preaching. It is sad, but true, that preachers have sometimes sought to justify poor preaching in the name of faithfulness. Danny Akin, President of Southeastern Baptist Theological Seminary says that preaching in a boring fashion is a sin. He says that the Word must not only be preached faithfully, it must also be preached well.[56]

Prepared to Suffer for Faithful Preaching

But having duly noted that some excuse dry and stilted preaching in the name of faithfulness, we must also note that there have been multitudes of faithful preachers who have suffered rejection despite preaching well. There have been multitudes of preachers throughout the history of the church who have preached faithful and rich sermons with little appreciation from the people to whom they were sent. Faithfulness in preaching is not measured by whether or not it is popular. The world is full of preaching that is popular yet unfaithful to Scripture and hateful to God.

If a pastor is going to strive for an accurate handling of Scripture, there is a cost to be considered. He must be prepared, as a matter of conviction, to sacrifice his own popularity with people in order to be faithful to God and to His word. In a day of love for entertainment, and the desire for instant gratification, a well-reasoned sermon, regardless of its excellence and passion, may not fit the fancy of a particular crowd. The preacher's test, however, may not only be a crowd's desire for entertainment. The preacher may also meet with a people who desire to be left alone in their sin. The faithful preacher must be convinced in his own mind that to speak the truth of God's Word is more loving toward people than to give them words that entertain them, or empty words that affirm them.

To accurately convey a message that confirms godliness and confronts sin (as Scripture does) is difficult work. Avoiding the conflict Scripture brings is easy: remain vague. But if a preacher strives for accuracy in his handling of God's Word, vagueness will give way to a vivid message that is life to some and death to others (2 Cor 2:15-16).

A Lifetime of Learning

Finally, the price to be paid in the pursuit of accuracy in preaching includes the cost of learning. Accuracy motivates one to pursue the training that provides the tools necessary for that work. Whether that training is found in the local church by means of pastoral mentorship, or in the formal academic setting of the seminary, every preacher must pursue competency. Training in the biblical languages, the study of sound hermeneutical principles, instruction in theology, in church history, and guidance in sermon construction and delivery, are all pursued because of pastoral desire. If one desires to serve Christ well, and to serve His people well, then he assumes the place of a learner so as to become a better teacher. After receiving that training his work has just begun. Faithful preaching will mean a commitment to the discipline and hard work in the study that puts those tools to work for the good of the congregation. Good preaching is hard work. A faithful pastor will never be satisfied with the occasional sermon that has been well studied and carefully prepared. The faithful preacher provides good pasture week after week and sermon after sermon.

CHAPTER FIVE
PASTORAL PREACHING COURAGEOUSLY CARES FOR PEOPLE

Loving people pastorally is dangerous business. Faithful preaching–preaching that manifests a true affection for souls–will prove costly. The pastor who preaches with affection, as an ambassador of Jesus Christ, must also be armed for the adversity he will certainly face.

Affection and Pastoral Preaching

The one quality that makes pastoral preaching work is that of affection. If a preacher possessed every other quality that would make preaching effective, but did not love the people to whom he preached, he would not deserve the title pastor. Preaching must not be divorced from love. If the goal of preaching is love, then the source of preaching must also be love. Paul was clear that the goal of Christian instruction is love. "The aim of our charge is love that issues from a pure heart and a good conscience and a sincere faith" (1 Tim 1:5). It is no wonder, then, to see on the pages of the New Testament those who shepherded the churches overflowing with love as they instruct those churches.

In earlier chapters we touched on many texts that demonstrate the deep affection the shepherds of the New Testament church felt for the people of God. A few particular examples are offered here by way of reminder.

Paul's Affection for the Thessalonians

Paul's affection for the Thessalonian believers was expressed in a willingness, not only to impart the gospel to them, *but to impart himself*. These were not mere words for Paul. In fact, he was calling the Thessalonians to remember that this was what he and his associates actually did. "So, being affectionately desirous of you, we were ready to share with you not only the gospel of God but also our own selves, because you had become very dear to us (1Thess 2:8)." Gene L. Green, commenting on this passage, noted the rare language that Paul employed in communicating his affection to these people. He said, "The language Paul uses to speak of their love for the congregation is not found elsewhere in the NT, and is even rare in the literature of the era. The Greek term (*homeiromenoi*) means 'desire greatly' or 'long for,' a word found in such contexts as a funerary inscription that tells how the parents long for their deceased son."[57]

Paul's Affection for the Corinthians

Paul's love for the Thessalonians was not an isolated example. When battling for the hearts of the Corinthian believers he uses the same kind of comparison. He saw himself in the role of a parent when considering the spiritual need of the Corinthian church. He writes, "Here for the third time I am ready to come to you. And I will not be a burden, for I seek not what is yours but you. For children are not obligated to save up for their parents, but parents for their children. 15 I will most gladly spend and be spent for your souls. If I love you more, am I to be loved less? (2 Cor 12:14)."

There are several things to note in Paul's statement of love for the Corinthians. First, Paul indicates the enduring, persevering nature of his love for these people. This is now the third time he is willing to make his way to them. Second, he makes plain that his motives toward them are pure. He does not care about what they can give to him, he cares for them. Third, the perspective he has of his responsibilities and theirs mirrors that of a parent and a child. Fourth, what Paul is called to be and to do for these people is a matter of delight to him. His love for them is a matter of gladness. Fifth, what he is willing to give to them goes beyond anything material. He is willing to expend himself on behalf of their souls. Finally, he loves them even if he is not loved in kind, yet he will make use of his love for them as he appeals for a reciprocated affection.

These examples are among many found in the New Testament. They illustrate the pastoral love that stood behind the preaching and teaching of the New Testament leaders. They also illustrate the fact that such love is brought to bear upon the consciences of those being instructed. The apostle's teaching of these people, and his ability to correct them, includes an appeal to his personal relationship with them, his personal example of sacrifice on their behalf, and to a God given affection for them.

Pastoral Affection in Contemporary Church Philosophy

Such examples are far removed from what is often found in the mindset expressed and touted by many contemporary pastors. Church ministries are often described as if the church is simply a gathering place for people looking for a religious fix. In many cases there is no distinction drawn between the person who simply shows up for the Sunday gathering and a person who would be considered a member of the church. What this means, of course, is that a genuine conversion, biblical baptism, and the willingness for mutual accountability that should exist in a church, is never really stressed. A serious approach to church membership considers these things, along with a clear understanding of things like doctrinal agreement. But in contemporary church growth schemes, church membership is either rarely mentioned, pushed far into the background of the church's life, or been jettisoned altogether.

This approach to ministry witnessed in many churches insures a ministry that is largely impersonal. The preacher has no real knowledge of the spiritual condition of the people to whom he preaches. He does not relate to them as a parent would to a child. He is not someone who imparts himself along with the message that he preaches. Rather, he relates to them as a CEO would to a customer. He relates to a congregation like someone who sells goods to a people who are thought of as consumers and product at the same time. He sells his goods to them and then uses the number of people who buy the goods as evidence that one should buy into the product made up of those who attend. The large gathering is itself a vital part of the product. "If you want a place that is exciting and offers many things that smaller churches cannot offer, then come be a part!"

Many of the largest so-called ministries of our time are often the poorest examples of what affection in preaching is supposed to be. The absence of a shepherd's affection is evident in the shallow content of the preacher's sermons and the shallow concern for the spiritual condition of those who listen to him. Instead of preachers who would gladly spend and be spent on behalf of souls, we find preachers making merchandise of souls as they promote themselves.[58]

Ambassadorship and Pastoral Preaching

Pastoral preaching includes the concern for evangelism. A pastor preaches to the church, but he never ceases to do the work of an evangelist (2 Tim 4:5). Pastoral preaching understands that the people of God were not only brought into being through the gospel, they live their lives out of the gospel. Biblical preaching recognizes that the church is formed through the preaching of the gospel. The pastoral preacher loves the church in advance.

A love for the church includes a love for those who have yet to be added to the church. A right understanding of the doctrine of election, far from cooling evangelistic zeal, drives evangelistic zeal. Christ died for a people who are now being gathered in as the gospel is faithfully proclaimed. An understanding of that ingathering means that the gospel preacher can endure suffering in the confidence that where the gospel is faithfully proclaimed, souls will most certainly be saved.

Paul's understanding of this is reflected in the pastoral epistle of 2 Timothy. He writes, "Remember Jesus Christ, risen from the dead, the offspring of David, as preached in my gospel, 9 for which I am suffering, bound with chains as a criminal. But the Word of God is not bound! 10 Therefore I endure everything for the sake of the elect, that they also may obtain the salvation that is in Christ Jesus with eternal glory (2 Tim 2:8–10)."

It seems clear that Paul's view of salvation, here, includes more than just conversion. As he endures suffering he concentrates on that final salvation that will be manifested in a day of eternal glory (v.10). In this way it can be argued that Paul's endurance serves the church as an example of faith in a coming day of triumph and the endurance that exists in that hope.

But one cannot exclude, in Paul, a confidence in the conversion of lost humanity based on God's electing purposes. His statement about endurance for the sake of the salvation of God's elect (v.10) is tied to his statement about the impossibility of chaining the Word of God (v.9). Some might think that by imprisoning Paul, the influence of the preaching of the gospel is stopped. Paul expresses his confidence that no such thing is possible. It is his confidence in the unstoppable nature of the gospel that fuels his endurance. He is confident that his preaching of the gospel, and the preaching of others emboldened by his example, will lead to the salvation of those destined by God to belong to His people.

In this way the heart of a pastor and the heart of an evangelist are joined together. Evangelism is the means God uses to form the church of Jesus Christ. Faithful preaching will mean the conversion of sinners, and the conversion of sinners will mean souls added to the church (Acts 2:41–42; 5:14). The preacher with a pastor's heart walks in the example of His own shepherd. The Chief Shepherd's voice did not only comfort and instruct those who were already following Him. Jesus' shepherd's heart looked upon the multitudes of lost people and felt compassion (Matt 9:36). It was a shepherd's heart that grieved for the unbelieving (Matt 22:37). It was by means of the Shepherd's preaching work that the sheep heard His voice and followed Him (John 10:16, 27). As it was with the Chief Shepherd so it must be with His undershepherds.

The faithful preacher also understands that until eternity reveals the genuineness of all professions of faith, the local church on earth will be spiritually mixed. The parable of the wheat and tares makes plain that this will be true in the current age (Matt 13:24–30). Churches that are faithful to the gospel take great care to ensure that those who are admitted as members of the church have a credible profession of faith in Christ. But regardless of how diligent the examination of candidates for membership, the church will always witness the tragedy of apostasy. If the New Testament letters reveal such a tragedy, then churches today can be sure that they will have to deal with it as well. This means that a preacher is faithful to think about those who need to be converted among the group gathered on Sunday. Though it is to be granted that Spurgeon's ministry was a unique one, his concern for evangelistic fruit in the ministry of a preacher must not be dismissed. He decried the men who were able to continue at ease in preaching when they saw no conversions year after year.[59]

An evangelistic concern does not mean, however, that the pastoral preacher must adopt a different preaching *method* in the interest of evangelism. Rather, the preacher is *mindful* that lost people sit before him in any given church service. He is full of desire to see people converted to Christ. As Spurgeon said, "If the Lord gives you no zeal for souls, keep to the lapstone or the trowel, but avoid the pulpit."[60] When this evangelistic awareness and desire is present in the preacher it expresses itself in his prayer life in advance of the sermon. It will also express itself in the course of his preaching as he makes application of the biblical text.

Pastoral preaching, then, is not simply a man desiring to instruct the people who already belong to Christ. Without question, the careful instruction of God's people, the desire to see believers brought to maturity, is a priority (Col 1:28). The preacher who manifests the heart of the Chief Shepherd always has an eye toward those who are not yet reconciled to God, and longs to see them gathered in.

Adversity and Pastoral Preaching

Believers have not only been chosen for faith in Jesus Christ, they have been chosen for suffering (Phil 1:29). The church's pastors are no different than the rest of their brethren in this matter. Pastors have not been exempted from suffering and often, in God's providence, will lead the way in suffering. The adversity that any faithful pastor can expect in this world can be described in at least two ways.

First, the preacher can expect adversity in the form of all the difficulties that are common to men. A man who is called to preach is not exempted from the troubles of life. Perhaps a young man entering the ministry could mistakenly believe that now all of his circumstances will cooperate with his desires to serve God's people. That same young man may suddenly find it seems just the opposite. He finds obstacles to his service, perhaps in the form of health challenges, or financial challenges, or unexpected issues that arise in his family. The loss of a child, his wife's cancer diagnosis, the continual strain of too much month and not enough money—what do these sorts of thing mean? Is he to conclude that God is displeased with him, or that his desire to serve in ministry is misguided? In truth, those providential troubles are often used by God to make the man more useful. If the troubles do not represent disqualifying sins in his life, and if he navigates those troubles faithfully (not perfectly), they are simply tools in the hand of God that further develop the man who preaches His word. If the captain of our salvation was destined for trouble and sorrows, and if God used those troubles and sorrows (even to the point of death on the cross) to perfect Him (Heb 2:5–18), then the pastor must not be surprised by suffering.

In the case of Christ, His sufferings were designed by the Father to identify Him with us. The perfecting work spoken of by the writer of

Hebrews had nothing to do with moral deficiency. There was nothing that needed to be added or subtracted from the life of Jesus in the moral realm. Jesus was perfectly holy. Rather, the perfection spoken of by Hebrews was one that had to do with His mission and role as Savior. The Father led Jesus in a pathway that fulfilled everything that the Messiah was to be, and to do, for God's glory and for God's people.

We can look to our high priest and know that He has blazed the trail we must walk. In our temptations and tests we know that He has demonstrated the way of obedience through those same things.

R. Kent Hughes writes, "His being made 'perfect through suffering' has reference to his being made a *perfect pioneer of salvation*. The idea is that he was perfectly equipped to do the job."[61] If God prepared His Son for His role through suffering, the preacher must not be surprised when God prepares him for his role through suffering.

Life experience does not change what Scripture means. A young man, with little life experience, can be a good exegete. That same young man may be a good communicator. He may be especially gifted in the organization of the biblical material for the purpose of preaching. He may show evidence of a unique insight taught by the Spirit of God. But God knows that more is needed.

What God often does is lead a preacher through life in a way that the man gains an increasing personal experience in the message that he is called to preach. That experience makes a real difference in the life of the preacher and in the life of his preaching. God ordained that human priests would be compassionate toward the people whom they served (Heb 5:1–3). In a similar way, the preacher learns to shepherd people with gentleness as God humbles him and breaks him through the troubles of life. A man who knows his own need for patience and gentleness at the hands of God and others preaches the truth of God's Word in a way that reflects love. He also gains in the kind of experience that allows him to apply Scripture with greater exactness and skill in the matters of the heart. A doctor must learn patients as well as medicine. Likewise, a preacher must learn his church as well as the craft of his sermons.

With little life experience, a preacher's sermons (as accurate as they may be, and as much good as God does with them) may lack the human element. If God did not desire a human element in preaching, He would not have made use of human preachers. God works in the preacher's life (through troubles) to teach wisdom, maturity, and union with his hearers. Through the circumstances of life, the preacher shares in the lives of those to whom he preaches and grows in affection for them. Of course, no preacher will ever experience *everything* that every church member lives through, but the troubles he does experience will serve to make him more caring with respect to the troubles that are unique to others. After all, there are common elements that make up every trial and temptation (1 Cor 10:13).

The second form of adversity has already been touched on numerous times throughout this chapter. *Faithful preaching will eventually mean adversity in the form of human opposition.* Every faithful preacher must be armed with readiness for suffering (1 Pet 4:1–4). This form of adversity will also make a major contribution to a man's preaching ministry. Our Lord had His Judas. Paul had his Demas who deserted him (2 Tim 4:10). Paul also knew pain and trouble at the hands of Alexander the Coppersmith who did him "much harm" (2 Tim 4:14). There was also Hymenaeus whom Paul had to hand over to Satan (1 Tim 1:20). The Corinthian church broke Paul's heart (2 Cor 6:11–13).[62]

If one is not prepared for adversity, both in life and in the way of preaching, then he will be sorely disappointed. Knowing these things and living these things are very different. God makes the one (knowing) into the other (living) by His sovereign and loving direction of our lives.

Part Two Conclusion

When I write about pastoral preaching I am not writing about a particular method for preaching, but rather a God-ordained mindset for preaching. When that mindset is present it will be manifested in ways I have described. There will be a proper sense of authority, accountability, and adoration. There will be a commitment to accuracy, affection for the people, and faithfulness to the work of ambassadorship. All of these things will be forged and proven in the furnace of adversity. These things belong to pastoral preaching, they express pastoral preaching, and they are used by God to make a preacher a better shepherd as God progressively forms the man who preaches His Word.

PART THREE

THE STABILITY FOR PASTORAL PREACHING

CHAPTER SIX
THE DOCTRINE OF PERSONAL CALLING

Holy Scripture reveals that God is the one who makes preachers (Eph 3:7). It is therefore clear that training alone could never achieve such a thing. A man can have a head full of knowledge about preaching and not have the God-given ability to do it. God equips preachers for their task and empowers them in their work. He ordains them to preach His word and therefore prepares them for their unique service. Just as a commanding officer makes certain his troops have the necessary equipment to complete their mission, so God provides the necessary equipment for the preacher's assignment. Scripture also provides evidence that when a man knows God has called him to the task of preaching, that knowledge provides a stable footing for the difficult times that will surely come.

What follows are some observations about the equipment God grants to those who preach His word. These are points for a preacher's self-examination, and they would serve those who must examine others for the preaching office. Without the firm conviction that God has assigned us the task of preaching, we will not be prepared to face the inevitable hard times that come in the course of ministry. Without the firm conviction that the man who preaches to the church has been chosen by God for the task, the church will not find confidence in his ministry during challenging seasons. Knowing how God equips His preaching servants, then, is vital for both the preacher and the church. It provides a pathway for testing that is essential for the men who preach the word and for those who must sit under their ministry.

Personal Calling

The proper equipment for preaching begins with a divine call. If a man is not called to preach, regardless of his other talents, he should never be in the role of one who gives his life to preaching. It is important to define what is meant by a call to preach.

The Call to Preach Defined

The call to preach is most simply described in the terms of choice or appointment. A call to preach means that a man has been chosen to preach. This is vital and is the all-encompassing way to describe the call to preach. It means that in an ultimate sense he has not taken up preaching on his own. The church has not made him a preacher, nor has any individual made him a preacher. He is not self-made; he is not community-made; he is not institutionally-made; he is chosen by God for his spiritual service. This qualification, understood in an ultimate sense, is an important one. Though God has chosen the man for this task, God makes use of multiple influences in the formation of the preacher. God makes use of the community of the saints, and He makes use of institutions. Even so, the man who is called to preach is able to know that the task of preaching is one that has been assigned to him by God.

This definition of a call to preach, that emphasizes choice or appointment, can be expanded to include divine enablement and personal development. The man who has been chosen by God for preaching has been *gifted* in a way that allows him to carry out the task. That same man must meet the biblical *character qualifications* for church leaders. His personal character, desire for the task, and the manifest giftedness for the work, identify him as a man called by God. To imagine that God has chosen a man for preaching whom He has not gifted for that work, and who is not pursuing Christ in an honest fashion, is a vain imagination.

A Call to Preach Illustrated

On the pages of Scripture, many servants of God have expressed confidence that they were chosen by God for a particular role in ministry. Paul was able to say he was appointed a preacher (1 Tim 2:7, 11). Moses had confidence that his task was one the LORD had assigned to him (Num 16:28–30). Paul encouraged Timothy by reminding him of his gift, which was confirmed by the laying on of hands (1 Tim 4:14; 2 Tim 1:6). There are many other examples that could be offered.[63] A similar kind of confidence, though not based in the same kind of dramatic manifestations as those experienced by prophets and apostles, has been expressed by many throughout the history of the church.

John MacArthur, in an interview concerning preaching, described his own personal sense of calling. MacArthur said, "I am, above all things, a preacher. I could give up everything tomorrow. I could walk away from radio. I really do not care. If the Lord wants me to do that, that's fine. I do not need to write another book. I do not need to be a president of an institution. I do not need any of that, but I cannot live if I do not preach.

It is not that I am driven by the crowd to do that. It is not external. I am driven internally to do that. This is a calling upon my life. It is almost an inexplicable drive within me. It is work to preach, as you well know. It is work to prepare, but I do it, and I do it with a certain joy. Sometimes I stand up, even now, after all these years, and I walk around because I am overwhelmed by what I have just discovered or seen. It is an internal drive that is the heart of a calling. It is not because I can do it. It is not because I can communicate, have skill at communication, or because people like to listen to me. It is internal. Sometimes people say, 'Well, you came to our church, and we just have a little church and it is so nice of you to come.' That is irrelevant to me. It is not about them. It is about me. It is about this passion internally to deliver the Word of God. That is what drives me. That is who I am. Every book I have ever written started as a sermon. Every commentary I have ever written started as a sermon. In fact, I have other jobs, and what I do is meet with people and preach at them."[64]

A Call to Preach Distinguished from General Responsibilities

This calling should be distinguished from the general responsibilities entrusted to every Christian. Every believer is called to preach the gospel in the sense of evangelism. Any believer may preach the Word of God when given the opportunity to instruct other believers.[65] But a man who is meant to *give his life* to preaching, a man who is meant to be a teacher to the Lord's church as a pastor-teacher (Jas 3:1; Eph 4:11), is a man who has been specifically gifted and prepared by God for that purpose. Such a belief in a divine call to ministry is nothing new. Church history reflects the conviction that a man who is to give his life to preaching is a man who was made for preaching. From his mother's womb he was set apart for the task. The work of preaching is what God ordained for him from all eternity. He was chosen for salvation and for the role he would assume in God's kingdom work (Gal 1:15–16). But as will be seen, such a belief is far from uncontested.

Differing Viewpoints on the Doctrine of Calling

In recent times, there seems to be increased skepticism regarding a particular call to preaching. The idea of a special call to ministry, and especially a call to the ministry of preaching, has been disputed or ignored. More and more it seems acceptable to think, "We are all called to ministry, we are all called to declare the Word of God, and therefore the work of preaching does not require any additional call." The approach seems to be that if someone desires to make ministry his life's work, he must simply be sure that the biblical character qualifications are met (1 Tim 3:1–7; Titus 1:5–9), and pursue the proper training and credentials. This skepticism regarding a specific call to preach comes from more than one quarter and takes more than one form.

The Call to Office View

Ed Stetzer is an example of someone who holds influence in the teaching and training of future pastors but rejects the concept of a "call to preach."[66] In a 2007 article for *Christianity Today* entitled "Is There Really a 'Call to Preach?" he answered in the negative. Stetzer sees more of an emphasis on a call to the office of elder than a call to preach.[67]

I affirm much of what Stetzer says in that article. There is no question that the office of an overseer requires an ability to instruct others in the faith. It is true that a faithful pastor having to work a job in addition to his work at the church, is no less legitimate when compared with others. Pastoring should never be viewed as a profession or vocation if those words are meant to indicate something that would be held in distinction from a high calling and biblical office.

But as Stetzer points out in that same article, a distinction is made among elders, in 1 Timothy 5:17, concerning those who labor in preaching and teaching. If all elders are devoted to preaching and teaching in the same way, then such a distinction would be unnecessary. And if all elders do not preach and teach in exactly the same way then the distinction must be one ordained by God Himself and would be the result of gifting. And if God has gifted a man to give his life to preaching, then preaching must be what God meant for that man to do. Such distinctions represent a reason to question whether a call to the office of elder equates to a call to preach.

The Dedicated to Preaching View

Contrast Stetzer's point of view with that of the famous London Baptist preacher Charles Haddon Spurgeon. In Spurgeon's *Lectures to My Students* he devoted an entire section to the "Call to the Ministry." In that section he says that preaching is analogous to prophecy. Spurgeon said, "In the present dispensation, the priesthood is common to all the saints; but to prophecy, or what is analogous thereto, namely, to be moved by the Holy Ghost to give oneself up wholly to the proclamation of the gospel, is, as a matter of fact, the gift and calling of only a comparatively small number; and surely these need to be as sure of the rightfulness of their position as were the prophets; and yet how can they justify their office, except by a similar call?"[68]

What makes Spurgeon's view somewhat confusing is that his views of eldership were more Presbyterian-like in nature. This allowed Spurgeon to unite a "call to preach" with a "call to pastor." He says of pastors, "When our Lord ascended on high he gave gifts unto men, and it is noteworthy that these gifts were men set apart for various works: 'He gave some, apostles; and some, prophets; and some, evangelists; and some, pastors and teachers' (Eph. 4:11); from which it is evident that certain individuals are, as the result of our Lord's ascension, bestowed upon the churches as pastors; they are given of God, and consequently not self-elevated to their position."[69]

Spurgeon clearly understood the pastors spoken of in Ephesians 4:11 as men who had a unique calling upon their lives for preaching. He made plain that he wasn't talking about someone who engaged in preaching occasionally, but to someone whose life is dedicated to the ministry of God's Word. He also made plain that such a man must be called by God, and no one should step into that role without the confidence that God has called him.[70]

Spurgeon would often use the terms pastor, overseer, and elder, in the same context. He did not, however, believe that all elders were called to preach by virtue of their call to the office of elder. For Spurgeon there was "the pastor" (a man called to preach), the elders, and the deacons. There may be more than one "pastor" or "minister" if the needs of a church dictated it, but he would have never concluded that all of the elders at Metropolitan Tabernacle were called to preach. In addition, even when the church decided on multiple occasions that the work was too much for Spurgeon, so that they elected a "teacher" to assist him, there was no confusion as to which man was the "governor."[71] Those "teachers" were recognized by the congregation in distinction from the elders. In the case of the first two men called to that position (John Collins and Thomas Ness), they eventually left the Tabernacle to serve as "pastor" to other churches.[72] In fact, at the Tabernacle, elders had one year terms, while the pastor and the deacons remained in place as long as qualified.[73]

Spurgeon and his congregation made a distinction between the "minister" or "pastor," and elders. The pastor was an elder, and in that way belonged to the body of elders, but a man was not the pastor by virtue of being an elder.[74] He saw a distinction between teaching elders and ruling elders. All elders have oversight in the spiritual care of the church but not all elders preach. A pastor (or minister) was one who was called to preach and gave himself to the work of preaching.[75]

Spurgeon's view, of course, does not determine what is right. The Word of God is the standard. It is, however, an example from more recent church history of how a revered pastor, and the church he served, could believe in a plurality of elders while not understanding the call to preach and the call to eldership as one and the same.

Martyn-Lloyd Jones expressed his own conviction about this point. He also believed in a distinction among elders that assigned the preaching and teaching role to the teaching elders (pastors and teachers).[76] Where Lloyd-Jones lands on this issue is agreeable, yet the argument he uses to make his point is a weak one. It does, however, represent another example of a preacher (Lloyd-Jones) who believed in a distinct "call to preach."

The Call to Ordinary Office View

Brian Borgman represents yet another view of "calling" when he presents a summary of, and supplement to, lectures presented by Albert Martin on a theology of preaching. In a work entitled *My Heart for Thy Cause*, there is a perspective of the call to ministry that seems to mediate somewhere between someone like Stetzer and the doctrine of calling held by someone like Spurgeon or Lloyd-Jones.

Borgman makes the point that the "calls" recorded in Scripture represent extraordinary offices. The argument is that the call to eldership is a call to an ordinary office whereas the call to a prophet or apostle was a call to an extraordinary office. The result is that the call to this ordinary office will not involve something like direct revelation or supernatural confirmation. God will not "speak" to the person who is being called, He has already spoken.[77] The way to discern whether or not one is called is for the person to engage in a sober self-judgment against the qualifications set forth in the appropriate sections found in the Pastoral Epistles. In addition to the qualifications lists found in those epistles, there are also the passages that describe the work of the office and the giftedness necessary to carry out that work. As a result, the person examining himself, or being examined by others, must also soberly weigh whether or not the necessary gifts are evident in his life and attempts at ministry. In other words, there is not so much a subjective, spiritual, personal sense of calling, but an objective, rational, collaborative sense of calling.

One particular qualification is that of desire (1 Tim 3:1). The examination Borgman envisions, then, would begin with a person's desire for the office of overseer. The examination process would include confirming his understanding of what the office entails, his sober self-assessment in the light of the qualifications, and a conscientious judgment about whether or not the necessary gifts are present. This would require not only his own assessment, but the concurrent judgment of those given such a responsibility (church leaders), those close enough to know him well (friends and family), and a church body that knows his life.

It is interesting, however, that Borgman seems hesitant to distance himself too far from a view such as Spurgeon's. He seems, in places, to indicate something of a subjective and experiential sense of a specific call to preach. He quotes Spurgeon when Spurgeon insists on a strong desire for preaching. Borgman favorably quotes Spurgeon to say, "We must feel that woe unto us if we preach not the gospel; the Word of God must be unto us fire in our bones, otherwise, if we undertake the ministry, we shall be unhappy in it, shall be unable to bear the self-denial incident to it, and shall be of little service to those among whom we minister."[78]

In addition to this subjective desire, Borgman notes the need for the requisite giftedness. Again, he appeals to Spurgeon when he writes, "It is interesting to note that Spurgeon would not admit men into the Pastor's College unless they were able to show some fruit in their preaching labors, thus illustrating this qualification."[79] Borgman seems to equate this ability for preaching with the office of pastor. "There is a clear and inescapable logical connection which exists between the pastoral office and the intention of Christ who gives men to fill it. Those whom Christ calls, He equips with the requisite gifts (Eph 4:8; Jer 3:15)."[80]

A Summary of the Views

Borgman, then, would seem to agree with Stetzer that all elders are called to preach (or at the least would be gifted teachers), would lay great stress on the objective and collaborative ways in which a man would be examined for the office, but would give a nod to Spurgeon or Lloyd-Jones on the need for the requisite sense of calling and fruitful evidence of giftedness for such a work. Stetzer would seem to reject a "call to preach" in favor of a "call to office." Spurgeon would reject the notion that all elders are called to preach. Borgman seems to adopt a view that would include elements of each.

Observations Concerning Actual Practice

It is fascinating to note how churches that differ on the matter of church government still organize the responsibility of preaching in an almost identical fashion. Even those churches that would profess a belief in Stetzer's position, − a position that views a "call to preach" with skepticism − with rare exceptions, have a primary preacher. And in those same churches, even when preaching duties are shared, they are rarely shared among more than two or three men. In other words, while all of the elders engage in a spiritual ministry to the church (when elders are rightly conceived of), it is almost never the case that all of the elders engage in the *regular* labor of preaching. Even if such a rotational approach to preaching were practiced it would have to be admitted that this would be a historical anomaly.

It may well be contended that the usual practice of a primary preacher in churches is actually reflective of the will of the Holy Spirit. This is why, with respect to the organization of preaching responsibilities, churches look so similar despite their differences in ecclesiastical polity. Whether one looks at some congregational models that recognize a single pastor, or a model that recognizes a preaching pastor among the elders, or a Presbyterian model that distinguishes between ministers and elders, or a Bible Church model that recognizes the terms elder, overseer, and pastor as interchangeable, it is most often the case that a primary preacher exists in the congregation. If the church is larger there may be multiple pastors who preach on various occasions, but even then, there is normally a primary preacher with others in the elder body who preach less often.

This is actually (whether a church and its leaders are cognizant of it or not) a mute testimony to the reality that a "call to preach" is not a delusion.[81] The church has historically practiced an approach to preaching that recognizes a unique calling and giftedness for that work. And churches have practiced this even when they have professed a different view. When one walks back along the pathway of church history, and examines the great men of God, the great churches of God, and the great movements of God, you will find great preachers of God. And you will find in those great preachers of God the testimony that they felt "called of God," not just to an office, but to the work of preaching itself.

Mark Dever is an example of someone who understands the terms elder, overseer, and pastor, as referring to the same office. Yet he also recognizes that while all elders must be able to teach (1 Tim 3:2), there is a unique role reserved for the one who is meant to preach the Word of God. And he does not shy away from calling that man the pastor.[82]

This is a part of the fascination referred to earlier. Those striving to be faithful to understand and describe what we see in Scripture, and what we practice in our churches, reveal this ongoing difficulty with terms. On the one hand there is a willingness to say that there are three New Testament descriptions for the same office, and yet visit almost any local church and there is some acknowledgement of a man set apart for preaching. Some may call him "the pastor," some the "senior pastor," some the "minister," some the "pastor-teacher," some the "lead pastor," some the "preaching pastor," but there is something that consistently unites all of these titles. God's people recognize that there is a primary man (in most cases) in their midst who is made for the proclamation of the Word of God. They not only recognize this; they usually desire it. This serves like a profound admission (even if an unwilling one) that a call to preach is real.

But what of these biblical terms (elder, overseer, and shepherd)? What is the right way to understand them? And can a firm biblical case be made for a doctrine of calling with respect to the work of preaching? To answer these questions, we will focus first on two key texts that point to a legitimate distinction that may exist in a body of elders based upon the ministry of biblical proclamation. Afterward we will broaden our examination to focus on several biblical arguments that will make the case for the reality of the "call to preach." Finally, some ways to discern a call to preach will be considered.

CHAPTER SEVEN
THE CALL TO PREACH AND 1 TIMOTHY 5:17

The fact that the New Testament churches were governed by a plurality of elders is disputed by some, but the biblical evidence is quite strong. Dever rightly recognizes that a plurality of elders in each local church was the New Testament practice, writing, "The New Testament never suggests a specific number of elders for a particular congregation, but it clearly and consistently refers to the 'elders' of a local church in the plural (for example, Acts 14:23; 16:4; 20:17; 21:18; Titus 1:5; James 5:14)."[83]

The New Testament Descriptions for the Pastoral Office

Further, it must be understood that these elders hold an office described three ways in the New Testament. The terms elder (πρεσβύτερος) and overseer (ἐπίσκοπος) are used of the same man, the same office, in key texts having to do with the church's leadership (Titus 1:5, 7; Acts 20:17, 28). Alexander Strauch, after surveying J.B. Lightfoot's views on the subject, communicates Lightfoot's view that these two words are used interchangeably to refer to the same office. Strauch says, "I conclude with Lightfoot's classic evaluation: 'It is a fact now generally recognized by theologians of all shades of opinion, that in the language of the New Testament the same officer in the Church is called indifferently 'bishop' (*episkopos*) and 'elder' or 'presbyter' (*presbyteros*).'"[84]

Not only are elder and overseer used interchangeably, it is plainly stated that the work of these men is the work of shepherding (ποιμαίνω) the church (Acts 20:28). The three terms are used in reference to the elders of the church and their work in 1 Peter 5:1–2. The reason for more than one term to describe the men who are to lead the church is to emphasize the maturity (elder) that should characterize them, the governing task (overseer) that is assigned to them, and the nature of the governance that they exercise (shepherding).[85]

A Division of Duties in the Pastoral Office

Having established the truth of a plurality of elders in each church, and the interchangeable terms used to describe their office, one faces an important question. Does the plurality of eldership, and the requirement that all elders be able to teach (1 Tim 3:2), argue against a unique call to preaching that may distinguish some elders from others? Are Stetzer and others right when they prefer a "call to office" as opposed to a "call to preach?" To say it another way, is it wrong to think of some elders as having a unique call to preach, a calling not given to all of the elders? The first biblical text that sheds light on the question is 1 Timothy 5:17. It reads, "Let the elders who rule well be considered worthy of double honor, especially those who labor in preaching and teaching."

If ever a text indicated that there may be a division of duties within an elder body, this is one of them.[86] The apostle insists that elders who rule well are to be considered worthy of double honor. [87] What is noteworthy for the question being considered, however, is that he lays special stress upon a particular kind of elder. Of those who should be honored, the ones *especially* worthy are those who labor in the word and teaching.[88] As George Knight notes, this combination of word and teaching likely points to the activities of preaching and teaching.[89]

Elders Especially Devoted to Preaching and Teaching

Prior to thinking about the implications of this text, however, there is a crucial debate amongst commentators that we must look into. It has to do with the translation of the word μάλιστα (especially). Some contend that the word should not be translated "especially." Rather, they argue for an explanatory sense and therefore take it as "namely" or "that is." On this reading, the text would say something like: "Let the elders who rule well be considered worthy of double honor, *namely*, those who labor in preaching and teaching." [90]

How to Understand μάλιστα

The result of that reading is that one can argue that the Bible does not allow for a two-tiered view of eldership.[91] All elders do the work of preaching. It is not a division of duties that is envisioned, but an emphasis on those who carry out the duties in the most zealous fashion. Though all elders are the preachers and teachers to a particular church, those who do it well are those who are exhausting themselves in the ministry of proclamation. It may also be that the verse points to a situation where, though all elders do the work of preaching, only some of them are currently engaged in that work. Perhaps the difficulty of working to provide a living outside the church limits their teaching opportunities in the life of the congregation. Benjamin Merkle summarizes such a position when he writes, "It is also possible to translate the Greek word *malista* ('especially') as 'namely' or 'that is.' In this case, Paul is not making a distinction between those who rule well and those who, in addition to ruling well, also preach and teach. Rather, those who rule well are precisely those who teach and preach (i.e., Paul is stating that the elders rule well *by* their teaching and preaching). This interpretation seems to fit Paul's stress on the importance of teaching, and a threefold division of elders is hard to imagine (i.e., those who rule, those who rule well, and those who rule well and also preach and teach)." [92]

If Merkle and others are correct, and we are not to read μάλιστα as "especially," then 1 Timothy 5:17 does not provide such an apparent proving ground for a distinction among elders based on a call to preach. Merkle, however, does not rule out such a distinction even if μάλιστα is taken to mean "namely." Merkle expressed the possibility that the elders who rule well are those especially gifted by God to teach. He continued, "...even with this interpretation, a distinction can be made between two types of elders. If ruling well is defined by 'working hard at preaching and teaching,' then a distinction can still be made between those who rule well (i.e., preach and teach) and those who do not rule well (i.e., do not preach and teach). For example, Knight states that it is likely Paul 'is speaking of a subgroup of the 'overseers' that consists of those who are *especially* gifted by God to teach, as opposed to other overseers, who must all 'be *able* to teach.'"[93]

This is a strange conclusion. On the one hand the writer would not be using μάλιστα in its usual sense (a superlative of the adverb μάλα meaning "most of all, above all, especially, particularly"), but on the other hand would be making the very point that μάλιστα would accomplish if taken in its usual sense![94] In addition, it would require that the ones gifted to teach are categorized as those who "rule well." We are left, then, to understand the absence of such a gift as leaving an elder in the position of not ruling well.

Since Skeat, Merkle, Knight, and others are opting for an interpretation of μάλιστα that is not in keeping with its primary lexical definition it must be asked what drives that conclusion. At least one answer seems to be, as evidenced by Knight, that a theological concern has preceded this discussion of 1 Timothy 5:17. In 1 Timothy 4:10, a troublesome interpretive challenge led Knight to adopt this unique definition of μάλιστα. 1 Timothy 4:10 reads, "For to this end we toil and strive, because we have our hope set on the living God, who is the Savior of all people, especially of those who believe." Knight opted for "namely" instead of "especially" in that text.[95]

Having adopted that definition of μάλιστα in verse 10, Knight proceeded to take the same view in 1 Timothy 5:17. Knight and others follow Skeat when opting for this unique definition of μάλιστα. The appeal seems to be that such an understanding promises to remove difficulties with other problem texts. It seems that these interpreters desire to apply this novel view of μάλιστα wherever it promises to simplify the interpretation.

Schreiner, citing work done by Vern Poythress, demonstrates convincingly that what seems to be a persuasive case by Skeat turns out to be empty upon close examination. Virtually every example given by Skeat, both inside the New Testament and outside, proves to be flawed. Schreiner makes his case in a pointed fashion. He says that Skeat's notion about the meaning of μάλιστα must be rejected.[96]

Especially convincing, and decisive, is the sound principle indicated in Schreiner's assessment, that a new meaning for a word is not to be accepted "in ambiguous texts if an established meaning for the word makes sense in the text under consideration." Clearly, the established meaning of μάλιστα makes sense in 1 Timothy 4:10 and 1 Timothy 5:17. What Knight and others seem to struggle with is what the established meaning would leave as its conclusion.

Applying the Lexical Meaning of μάλιστα

Removing the novel understanding of μάλιστα (namely or that is) as a possibility in 1 Timothy 5:17 is significant for the question of whether or not a call to preach is legitimate. If μάλιστα is understood in its correct sense of "especially," then 1 Timothy 5:17 proves difficult for those who see a complete parity among elders.[97] If every elder is entrusted with the same work of preaching and teaching then this verse leads to some odd conclusions. One result of reading the text in this way is that it forces us to say that some elders can be worthy of honor even though they do not work as hard as others in the ministry of the Word. Remember, if the call to office imparts a preaching responsibility to all (because the work belongs to the office), then it would seem to follow that all should be equally committed to laboring at it.[98] Even if some elders taught in a more limited way due to outside responsibilities, or the absence of opportunity, it would not be an excuse for a diminished effort.

To be clear, we would be understanding the apostle to say that honor should be given to elders that do not work hard (κοπιῶντες) in preaching and teaching (though they were equally responsible to do so). We would then have to understand him to say, "But *really make sure* to honor those who *work hard* in the ministry of God's Word." It would be akin to saying that an elder who shepherds others but does not labor in the Word of God and teaching is still honorable. That conclusion *is* possible (and I believe correct), but not if one believes that the call to office equals a call to preach. If the call to office constitutes the call to preach, then such an elder would be working hard at only half of his God-given duty. Yet the apostle Paul would be saying that such an elder is still an example worthy of honor. Given this reading, the man who works hard at both aspects of the office would be especially worthy of honor. Such an understanding of the text would seem self-defeating.

The only legitimate way that elders could be considered to rule well while not laboring in preaching and teaching, is if we understand this verse to say that the church recognized a distinction among its elders that allowed for division of duties. In this understanding, the church would recognize that there are some among the elders who are gifted and called to devote themselves in a special way to the ministry of the Word. That is to say, while all elders must be able to teach, all elders are not laboring in preaching and teaching in the same way. Understanding the text in this way allows for an elder to be faithful as an overseer even when preaching and teaching in the corporate gatherings is not his primary assignment. Philip Ryken understands the verse in this way (a separate question from his views on calling). In his commentary on 1 Timothy he says, "To one degree or another, all the elders do all these things. But here a distinction seems to be made between two kinds of elders, what Presbyterians usually call 'teaching elders' (often referred to as 'pastors') and 'ruling elders' (or simply 'the elders'). Some elders labor as preachers. In the contemporary church they are usually full-time members of the church staff. Since they do the bulk of the public teaching, they are identified as *teaching* elders. The difficulty of their work is suggested by the word 'labor,' which is a term for strenuous effort. Ruling elders are 'able to teach' (see 1 Tim. 3:2), of course, but that is not their primary vocation. Most of them have full-time jobs outside the church, yet one important part of their life's work is to rule or to govern the spiritual affairs of God's household."[99]

To be clear, all elders are engaged in the shepherding of God's flock. All elders are to be men of whom it can be said that they were appointed by the Holy Spirit to serve as overseers to shepherd the church of God (Acts 20:28). So, they are all *called* by God to shepherd His sheep, and all elders carry out their shepherding work by means of the Word of God. It does not follow, however, that all elders are equally engaged in *the preaching work*.[100]

How Duties Are Determined

When 1 Timothy 5:17 is understood in this way, it not only points to the reality of a call to preach, it also points to the possibility of elders who are not called to preach. That is, as long as a man is able to teach the faith soundly and effectively (at the least in ways necessary to shepherd God's people individually) he is qualified to serve as an elder. This, of course, assumes that he meets the other qualifications.

To preach the Word of God faithfully requires a special devotion of time and energy. Preachers must give themselves to prayer and the rigorous study and preparation for sermons if the church is to be cared for properly. It is right that some among the elders would be set apart to devote themselves to such a task. Any other approach (apart from a rotational approach) would lead to the neglect of other shepherding responsibilities.

But on what basis would such a choice be made? The only proper answer would be giftedness and maturity. But if giftedness is the basis, this would point to a choice made by God. Such a choice by God indicates a unique purpose for those men. It returns the matter back to the reality of a call to preach that allows for a distinction even among men serving as elders. The division of duties among elders would be based on the ability to distinguish between function and giftedness. All elders must be able to carry out the shepherding functions by means of the Word of God, but all elders are not equally gifted for the public proclamation of Scripture.

The argument being advanced is that there is a unique call (and therefore giftedness) to publicly proclaim the Word of God, and to instruct with the Word of God. This calling belongs to *some* among those who are called to shepherd the Lord's church. In other words, there is a calling within a calling. The call to proclaim the Word of God stands distinct from the call to serve as an elder, even though the man gifted in this way serves as an elder.[101] Such an elder's call to preach is evidenced by a gift for the public instruction of the church with Scripture.[102] This does not negate the other qualifications necessary to serve as an elder; it is something additional. All elders must be able to teach, but an ability to *herald* Scripture is not a gift possessed by all elders.[103]

It should also be added that because the man is gifted in this way and meant for this work, God makes such a calling sensible to the man. The man desires such a work, and feels a holy responsibility to pursue it. It is this personal sense of God's calling that so many faithful preachers have described throughout the history of the church.[104]

Common Objections Answered

There are objections that can be raised. Someone could object, "All are equally called to preach and teach, but the needs of the church require a division of duties. Any one of the elders could give himself more to the preaching and teaching of the word. The elders simply make a decision about which of them is to labor in preaching and teaching." I would answer that if anyone thinks that the only distinction in preaching ability (among men qualified to be elders) is a matter of diligence and hard work, he reveals his ignorance of the work of preaching. Just working hard at preaching does not make one a preacher. Any mature Christian and any discerning congregation can recognize that. Even great godliness, joined with hard work, does not make a man a preacher. Many a godly man has mistakenly claimed a preaching gift for himself that the listeners did not find credible. We may insist on absolute parity all we want, but congregations demonstrate that the people of God recognize differences.

Someone may respond to this answer by pointing out that there are differences in gifting and ability even among men who have proven to be effective in preaching. "Could this not apply to all in an elder body? Could it not be true that all of the elders are called to preach but some are more gifted than others?" I would answer that though there are variations of giftedness among men who are called to preach, what they all share in common is the Spirit's blessing upon their efforts. It is true that one man designed by God for preaching may shine brighter than another who shares that same design. But what is also true is that a man designed for preaching is blessed in the ministry of preaching in a way distinct from those who are not. In other words, the man's gift is confirmed by spiritual fruit. There is not only the fruit of conversions, there is also the fruit of congregational edification. The gifting necessary for such a work means that the man has a divinely imparted ability to teach the Scriptures in a way that brings clarity in the minds of the listeners. The result of the gift is that God's people have the truths of Scripture opened to their minds, made sensible to their hearts, and impressed upon their consciences in a way unique to that giftedness. Without that giftedness a man may be thoroughly acquainted with Scripture, and well versed in theology, but the Spirit's working through a particular giftedness for imparting the Scriptures will be absent. This is not to say that the Spirit cannot, and does not, work through those not gifted for such a task, but that the gifting has been given for a reason, and makes a difference. And I insist that God's people instinctively know this.

It is true that there may be more than one man called to preach in an elder body. When this is the case, however, those who are called to preach have a desire to preach. That desire either requires the man who is called and gifted for preaching to share the pulpit regularly with another brother, challenge him to remain patient for a season of additional maturity, or impel him to move on to another field of service where his gift can be more useful. In large churches he may have preaching opportunities in other settings that allow him to be content when he is not the primary preacher.

Desire and godliness, by themselves, do not identify the man who is called to preach. There have been many men who have desired to preach but struggled mightily when attempting to preach regularly. There have been many who could effectively teach the Word of God in certain formal and informal settings, and would therefore be qualified to serve as an elder (assuming all of the other qualifications), but discovered that preaching was not meant to be their primary ministry. They could preach on occasion, but found (sometimes through hard experiences) that they starved churches when they attempted to serve as the primary preacher. The Lord's church has ears for the men called and gifted by the Spirit to serve as preachers. Churches that lack maturity and discernment may sometimes be mistaken in their judgments about a man's giftedness for preaching. However, the church is not wrong when believing that just because a man is put forth to preach, or puts himself forth, it does not necessarily follow that God made him for preaching.

There are men who were made to preach as their primary ministry and there are men who were not. Acknowledging that reality allows for a church to recognize and honor qualified elders, who are faithful to their task, but are not primarily devoted to the ministry of preaching and teaching. The work of preaching (in its regular course) is assigned to men who are especially made for that task by God's sovereign choice. And if one asks how such a view of eldership allows for special honor to be bestowed on those who labor in preaching and teaching (1 Tim 5:17), the answer points to another distinction in God's church.

The Reason for Special Honor

Those who labor in the preaching and teaching of God's Word are to be especially honored because the preaching and teaching of God's Word is given special honor. Those who serve the church as the primary preachers lead in the midst of their fellow elders.[105] They do so because their knowledge of Scripture, in conjunction with a giftedness for expression and application, often helps the entire elder body to apply biblical principles to the needs of the church. God has designed for His word to stand at the head of the life and ministry of His church. This is not a denial that Jesus is the Lord of the Church and preeminent in everything. Rather, it is the acknowledgement of the honor that Jesus desires to be given to the ministry of the Word of God. It is also an acknowledgement that the men called to preach to the church constitute a gift to the church (Eph 4:11). This is true of all elders, but especially of those who are called by the Chief Shepherd to feed the flock in a devoted way. It is God's concern for the primacy of the ministry of His word that calls for the special priority of double honor in the case of those who are especially devoted to instructing the church. The idea may be expressed in the following way. If a church only has the means to support one of its elders by supplying his livelihood, let it be the man who devotes himself to preaching.

Answering the Doubts of an Egalitarian Age

These ideas are hard for our contemporary culture to accept. We live in an egalitarian age. Distinctions, especially ones predetermined by God, bother people. It is telling that a Brethren-like model of eldership (no functional distinction among elders) seems to have grown in popularity at the very time that egalitarianism is on the rise. From my own vantage point, in churches that embrace such an approach, many of the men who are recognized as elders, and now wear the mantle of a minister of the word, lack both the gifting and the God-granted shepherding instincts necessary to be a good preacher. As egalitarianism has grown in our culture, a lack of respect for divine choice has grown with it. As the recognition of divine choice has diminished, so has the fear and trembling associated with entering the preaching office. Knox wept and refused to preach to the church until he was certain of being called. Spurgeon asked how men can run without knowing that they have been sent. The contemporary culture's answer seems to be to question whether anyone really sends, and whether anyone is especially sent.

Answering the Charge of Pride

What is particularly troubling about this doubt regarding a special call for preaching is that it is often promoted in the name of humility. The idea of an elder body without any functional distinctions is often held forth as a model that best expresses servanthood. In truth, it takes genuine humility to recognize that all are not made for the same task. God has distributed gifts in a way that requires functional organization among pastoral leaders. Such a recognition requires the humility among elders to allow the ministry of God's Word to take the lead. The one especially gifted to preach the Word of God has a unique function and responsibility in the life of the church, even though a plurality of men share in the work of shepherding the church.[106] Each elder is equally culpable for the work he has been assigned, but all elders do not have the same function or responsibility in an elder body. The distribution of gifts determines each one's role and therefore unique responsibilities.[107]

Equality does not rule out functional structure. It is not surprising, if we pay attention to God Himself, that there would be a functional order in a healthy body of elders. If there is functional submission in the Godhead (where there is perfectly pure love and fellowship), then functional distinctions in an elder body should be expected.[108]

It must be recognized that all believers are slaves of Jesus Christ. The Head of the church has every right to make distinctions among His people. He has every right to gift us in accordance with the way that He has ordained to make use of us. He has every right to place us into particular roles for service. Each of us must be willing to humbly submit to God's gifting choices, and then submit to one another in the fear of Christ.

Any argument against such an interpretation based on humility or servanthood betrays a misunderstanding of spiritual gifts. Such distinctions are never a reason for self-exaltation (1 Cor 12:21–25). Glory does not belong to us; glory belongs to God. We serve with whatever gift God has given us. He has gifted those who teach the church so that they may be expended on behalf of others, not for others to be expended for them (2 Cor 12:15). But like everything else that God does, spiritual gifts are ordered (1 Cor 12:28). True humility respects that order.

A Conclusion from 1 Timothy 5:17

In light of the meaning of μάλιστα in 1 Timothy 5:17, and the inescapable implications created by the emphasis of special honor assigned to those who preach the Word of God, a God-determined organization among elders is indicated. That distinction points to a unique giftedness and calling for preaching. All in the elder body shepherd the church by means of the application of Scripture. That is why all elders must be able to teach. That does not require, however, that all elders be gifted preachers. Some in an elder body are especially devoted to the more public proclamation of Scripture.

One final thing should be mentioned before examining the next text. What has been said of the preaching ministry in a body of elders is not true of the other ministries assigned to elders. That is, all elders are not required to give themselves to preaching, but no preaching elder opts out of the work of shepherding. There are many who have imagined that they have been called and gifted for preaching who have no interest or desire to shepherd people. They will often believe themselves to be gifted for preaching, but confess to no desire to involve themselves in the lives of those to whom they preach. In some cases, they may decide that itinerate preaching is their calling. Worse, they imagine they are meant to teach others how to preach who will love the church in the way they have not. The idea that God calls a man to preach who does not have the church in his heart is completely foreign to Scripture.

The spiritual gifts are given for the edification of the church. They are exercised within the context of the church and on behalf of the church.[109] It is true that the man who is tasked with preaching will spend many hours in study and preparation for preaching, and this limits (to some degree) his time to spend with people. But he still cares for souls in ways that require time outside of the study and apart from the pulpit ministry (Acts 5:42; 20:20). He does not do this reluctantly; he does this because the church is in his heart (1 Pet 5:2). In truth, when a man removes himself from such work he forfeits the true genius of preaching (it is pastoral), and opens himself to a life of pride. There is nothing like shepherding responsibility to reacquaint the preacher with his true smallness. When a man preaches outside the context of the difficult work of caring for souls, he removes himself from the challenges that keep him aware of his desperate need for God. It is right to ask whether the New Testament knows of any gift for preaching that is meant to operate outside the context of the ministry of the local church.[110]

CHAPTER EIGHT
THE CALL TO PREACH AND EPHESIANS 4:11-16

The second text that points to a particular gift for preaching (and therefore calling) is Ephesians 4:11–16, which explains the unity of the body of Christ and what Christ has done to insure the maturity and proper function of the church. It is in that context that Paul writes of Christ's gifts to His church in the form of gifted men. These men are ascension gifts from Christ, given in the interest of equipping the saints for the work that will lead to the church's unity and maturity. The work of these gifted men leads to the spiritual protection and stability of the church, and with the goal of conformity to Christ and nourishment from Christ (vs.12–16). These men can be described as Christ's gifts because they are the product of His saving work, and the result of the Spirit's sovereign assignment of spiritual giftedness (1 Cor 12:11). In other words, Christ produced them.

Four important questions will be considered from this text. Paul mentions the apostles, the prophets, the evangelists, the shepherds and teachers. Is his emphasis on the offices associated with such men, or on the men themselves? This becomes especially important in view of the fact that this is the only place in the New Testament where the noun ποιμήν (shepherd or pastor) is figuratively used to speak of someone who serves as a spiritual leader in the church.[111] The question to be considered in light of this fact, and the previous question, is whether the shepherds spoken of here are unique within a body of elders? That is, are all of the elders/overseers also shepherds in the sense that verse 11 describes? That question is tied to another. We will consider the possibility that the word *shepherds* in verse 11 is joined to the word *teachers*. Are there two categories of men being considered in verse 11(shepherds and teachers); or is one category being described – shepherd-teachers? Finally, someone like Borgman suggests that a calling to an extraordinary office must be distinguished from a call to an ordinary office. Does the fact that shepherds and teachers are gifts to the church along with apostles, prophets, and evangelists, shed any light on that claim? Each of these questions has some bearing on our understanding of a call to preach and whether or not all elders are called to preach in the same way.

Is Paul Describing Offices or Gifts?

A few general observations about this passage are in order before some specific questions are addressed. For one, the gifts under discussion are gifts from Christ.[112] The immediate context makes this plain. Second, these gifts are given to the church, and they are given for the development of the church. The gifts result in the equipping, growth, maturity, and stability of the church, and its conformity to Christ Himself (vs.12–16). This is an especially important observation to remember when considering people who claim a call to preach but the church is not the focus of their efforts. Third, Christ gave these gifts to His church in the interest of accomplishing a particular aspect of His plan to fill all things (vs.10). The church, then, plays a strategic role in the future and ultimate manifestation of the glory and rule of Jesus Christ. Christ gives gifted men (and therefore the giftedness appropriate to the role) to accomplish His work, in the life of His church, for His glory. This is a truth that informs the motives, the goals, and the standards for those who preach the Word of God to the church. Fourth, these gifts manifest the triumph of Christ. These gifts are described making use of the analogy of a victorious general distributing the spoils of battle (4:8; Psalms 68:18). These gifted men are given by the victorious Lord of the church. The church, then, and the men who serve the church, walk in the victory already accomplished by Jesus, share in the riches that He distributes, and will one-day give account to Him. Fifth, there are either four or five categories of gifted men that have been given by Christ to the church. What they all have in common (apart from the things already mentioned) is that they each engage in the proclamation of God's Word and represent a teaching form of leadership to the church. Finally, verses 11–16 form one long sentence in the Greek text. The gifted men are meant to be viewed in the context of the entire statement concerning the reason why they were given and the results envisioned.

The first specific question to be considered is whether the apostle Paul is describing offices or gifts in Ephesians 4:11. To state it another way, is the apostle describing gifted men who are equipped to serve the church in these various *functions*, or is he listing Christ-granted *offices* that godly men would then be called upon to fill? This is an important matter for the question of calling. If these are gifted men (who are only able to serve the church in these ways because of unique Spirit-imparted abilities) then the giftedness is separate from any office. This would mean that pastor-teachers (or pastors and teachers) are gifted men who would be designed by Christ to serve the church in the office of elder, as opposed to the office of elder constituting the pastor-teachers.[113] This would not mean, however, that it would necessarily follow that all elders would be gifted as pastor-teachers. As has been stated many times already in this book, this is not a denial that all elders must be able to teach and to refute error (1 Tim 3:2; Titus 1:9). Rather, it would simply acknowledge that some are especially gifted for a shepherd-teaching role. In addition, the way that this gift is described would identify the heart of the biblical mindset and manner for preaching to the church. They would be described as shepherd-teachers, that is shepherds who engage in a ministry of instruction—shepherds who teach.

The answer to the question as to whether Paul is describing offices or gifted men seems quite apparent. It is clear that the gifts in this passage are the men themselves. Each category of gifted men is identified with a preceding article and a plural description of the men who constitute Christ's gifts. The last two plural nouns (shepherds and teachers) are governed by a single article. Harold Hoehner argues that the articles are being used as demonstrative pronouns. Hoehner says, "The article (τοὺς) is used as a demonstrative pronoun and can be translated 'some.'... each gifted person listed (e.g., τοὺς μὲν ἀποστόλους) is a predicate accusative and could be translated either 'some apostles' (AV), 'some as apostles" (NASB), or 'some to be apostles' (RV, ASV, RSV, NEB, TEV, JB, NIV, NJB, NRSV). The last translation is preferred because it brings out the distinction that each gifted person has a particular function among the assembly of believers. Each is to function in the measure of the gift given (vs.7)."[114]

The KJV, NASB, and NET translations treat the articles in this way. If the articles are to be taken as demonstrative pronouns, then the emphasis (as Hoehner points out) on each gifted person is unmistakable. Even if this reading is rejected, the context still points to the emphasis on giftedness rather than office. The entire section, beginning at verse 7, focuses on functional gifts not church offices.

Are Two Gifts Described by Shepherds and Teachers?

As already noted, the last two nouns of verse 11 (shepherds and teachers) are governed by a single article and may well form a unit.[115] But even if this cannot be established on grammatical grounds, I believe the preponderance of the evidence supports it. Though the noun ποιμήν is only used here to refer to men who would serve as ministers to the church, the shepherding verb ποιμαίνω seems to be used as the primary way to describe the responsibility of elders (1 Pet 5:1; Acts 20:28). As we have already noted in an earlier chapter, the shepherding task places special emphasis on the responsibility to feed the flock (John 21:15–17).

A similar list of gifts occurs in 1 Corinthians 12:28. The order of the gifted men is the same. The difference is that evangelists are not mentioned, and the word pastor or shepherd is not mentioned. It reads, "And God has appointed in the church first apostles, second prophets, third teachers..." It is true that none of these lists are intended to exhaust the ways in which Christ has gifted His church. It does seem, however, that "teachers" in 1 Corinthians 12:28 may be describing the same gifted man as the "pastor-teachers" since those who serve the local church as leaders are shepherds who teach. In other words, the "shepherding" aspect of the man would be assumed in 1 Corinthians 12:28 and made explicit in Ephesians 4:11.[116]

Lending weight to our conclusion about 1 Corinthians 12:28 is the fact that James describes teachers in a way that clearly assumes an authoritative and highly responsible role. He wrote, in James 3:1, "Not many of you should become teachers, my brothers, for you know that we who teach will be judged with greater strictness." First, the kind of accountability envisioned here, while true on some level any time a person teaches Scripture, clearly seems to be addressing those who would teach the church in an official capacity. Second, James includes himself among the teachers when he writes, "we who teach." Certainly James served in the role of an elder. The Greek construction allows for "pastors and teachers" in Ephesians 4:11 to be seen as one category of gifted men. The rest of the evidence—the shepherding function tied to the teaching function throughout the New Testament, the absence of pastors in the list of 1 Corinthians 12:28, and the word teachers used to describe church leaders in James 3:1—gives good reason to see the last two nouns of Ephesians 4:11 as shepherd-teachers.[117]

Are all Elders Pastor-Teachers?

The shepherd-teachers of Ephesians 4:11 are men given to the church to instruct the church. Each of the gifted men mentioned—the apostles, the prophets, the evangelists, and the shepherd teachers—are proclaimers of the Word of God. Each of these categories of gifted men represents a unique role in the life of the church, but the common denominator is that they are preachers. They are gifts from Christ because they are gifted by Christ. These are not *offices* being described but *men who are especially gifted for the offices.* Christ, by saving these men and by the sovereign distribution of spiritual gifts, prepares and fits these men for their unique roles in the life of the church.

Their teaching ministry is evidenced by what follows in Ephesians 4:12–16. Paul gives a big picture lesson. It is not a lesson about what is given to each church for the rest of time, but what has been given to the church viewed as a whole. The apostles and prophets are of a temporary nature. Together they served as the foundation for the church (Eph 2:19, 3:4; Rev 18:20). The order of the gifts, both here and in 1 Corinthians 12:28, point to the way in which the New Testament truth made its way into the life of the church. The apostles and their close associates were used to transmit the doctrine entrusted to the church (Acts 2:42; 1 John 4:6; 1 Cor 14:37). The prophets supported and supplemented the ministry of the apostles through exhortation and instruction that was probably more practical in nature (1 Cor 14:3). The ongoing instruction of the church is left to the evangelists and the shepherd-teachers. The apostles' doctrine is now the standard—inscripturated in the New Testament canon—and it is the material (along with the Old Testament Scriptures) that the evangelists and shepherd-teachers proclaim.

The noun εὐαγγελιστής is used only three times in the New Testament. Philip is called an evangelist (Acts 21:8). Timothy is told to do the work of an evangelist (2 Tim 4:5). Ephesians 4:11 is the third reference. Little information is given about the function of evangelists, but from the information given it can be said that they preached the gospel. Philip's ministry as well as Timothy's indicates that they evangelized those who would take their place in local churches. Timothy, at least, had a hand in shepherding churches in their infancy. Titus was involved in seeing permanent leadership established in the churches (Titus 1:5). That the Pastoral Epistles were addressed to Timothy and Titus indicates that they must have been involved in the same kind of ministry. The contemporary use of these gifted men is probably represented by ministry in the realm of missions, church planting ministry, and serving alongside shepherd-teachers in local churches. When stationed in local churches they lead the congregation in evangelistic training and proclamation. Just as a gifted pastor-teacher does not excuse the rest of the elders to neglect the function of teaching, so the gifted evangelist does not excuse the pastor-teachers from the work of evangelism.

The shepherd-teachers primary work is that of διδασκαλία (teaching). They teach the church as they proclaim (κηρύσσω) the Word of God (2 Tim 4:2). All of these men (apostles, prophets, evangelists and shepherd-teachers), collectively, are used by the Lord of the church to accomplish the things described in verses 12–16. As the gifted men proclaim the Word, the saints are equipped to do the work of the ministry, so that the church is built up (vs.12). The church is brought to a unity of the faith, to a knowledge of Jesus, to a full-grown man, into conformity with Christ (vs.13). The result is that the church is delivered from immaturity (vs.14), from instability (vs.14), and led into truth centered conformity to Christ and edification in love (vs.15–16). Each kind of gifted man plays the part that God designed for the maturity and stability of the church, and the glory of His Son. The apostles and prophets were at the forefront at the beginning, the evangelists and shepherd-teachers carry on the work after the foundation was in place.

The point to be made with respect to the question of whether all elders are pastor-teachers is to recognize that these are gifted men (especially equipped by God) not offices. Either every elder is to be a shepherd-teacher, so that every elder is a man uniquely gifted to shepherd and instruct the Lord's church. Or one or more of the elders is a shepherd-teacher, especially gifted for proclaiming God's Word, and the other elders shepherd the church with them. All elders must be able (due to the knowledge of Scripture and spiritual character and maturity) to carry out the function of teaching necessary for the work of oversight.

1 Timothy 5:17 clearly indicates that some elders have a ministry of preaching and teaching that differs from other elders. That distinction

points to the truth that all elders must be able to teach, but all elders are not equally gifted for preaching and teaching. The shepherd-teachers are the preachers given to congregations and are distinguished by giftedness from those in the elder body who do not possess that giftedness. While all elders, regardless of giftedness, are called to shepherd the church with the Word of God, some elders have a unique calling and giftedness for proclaiming the Word of God in a more public and regular way. Thus, Ephesians 4:11, taken together with 1 Timothy 5:17, points to the reality of a call to preach.

Does Calling Differ Based on the Extraordinary Offices vs. the Ordinary Offices?

The final question that Ephesians 4:11 raises is whether Borgman is right in a firm division between the kind of call that might be expected in the case of an extraordinary office and that which belongs to an ordinary office. Borgman is actually helpful in his treatment of the subject. His position, and the one championed in this chapter, would only differ in the strength of emphasis placed on certain aspects of the conversation.

Borgman rightly notes that the subject of a call to the pastoral office belongs to the realm of "experimental divinity or the theology of Christian experience."[118] By that statement he acknowledges the personal and experiential nature of discerning God's call to ministry. He notes that viewpoints held on the question vary along a spectrum of thought, using Spurgeon and R. L. Dabney as his polar examples. He mentions this in a series of cautionary principles to bear in mind when formulating one's understanding of a call to ministry. He exhorts his readers to be careful of simply choosing one person's (such as Spurgeon or Dabney) perspective on the matter. Then, to safeguard against being led astray by experience, he draws a firm line between the call that would belong to an extraordinary office and an ordinary one. He distinguishes the two as he writes, "Another foundational principle is that this subject must be approached with the full awareness that the consideration is for the call to an ordinary and not an extraordinary office in the church. The Bible is full of extraordinary calls to extraordinary offices, such as those to Elijah, Isaiah, Jeremiah and Paul. When hammering out a biblical theology of the call, it is a mistake to think that one's call needs to be similar to that of an Old Testament prophet or a New Testament Apostle. There have always been those willing to get on a horse and see what happens, but those Damascus road calls are extraordinary because they are for an extraordinary office. A pastor's call is an ordinary call to the ordinary office."[119]

How will these two kinds of calling differ? Borgman follows by saying, "While the call of prophets and apostles was by special revelation, that of the gospel minister may be termed a scriptural call."[120]

Ephesians 4:11 gives a strong reason to pause on Borgman's thesis. For in that verse evangelists and shepherd-teachers are described as Christ's gifts to the church in the very same context as apostles and prophets. Though two of these gifted types of servants belong to the foundation of the church, and two belong to the ongoing life and ministry of the church, they are treated in exactly the same way. Certainly it could be argued that the reason for this is because at the time Ephesians was written all four types of gifted men were still in existence. Nonetheless, the fact that they are not firmly distinguished in Paul's description is still informative. Each kind of man is a gift to the church from Jesus Christ. Each kind of man is explained by Christ, by virtue of His sovereign will regarding the distribution of individual gifts. There is no difference between these men on that level.

Where Borgman is certainly right is in the idea that a call to preach in the era beyond the apostolic age is not confirmed in revelatory ways. No preacher today will have a Damascus road experience. No preacher today will meet with angels who will confirm God's will for him. No preacher today will meet with God in a wind, or an earthquake, or in an audible voice.

But where he may press too far is in his explanation for the absence of revelatory confirmation. The reason for a difference in how God makes His calling sensible in the times of prophets and apostles as compared with contemporary times, has less to do with the office itself and more to do with the era that the office belongs to.

The fact that Paul could deal with gifted men who would hold temporary offices in the same breath he deals with men would hold permanent offices, would seem to indicate that he saw them as similar. In truth, calling is determined by God's choice and by God's equipping work in a man's life. He destines men to preach the Word of God while assuming a particular role in the life of the church. He equips those men with the necessary giftedness and with the necessary development. This does not differ whether it is an apostle, or a prophet, or an evangelist, or a shepherd-teacher being considered. God chose Paul, saved Paul, gifted Paul, and prepared him for the way He intended to use him. God chooses men to preach His Word today. He saves them, He equips them with a spiritual gift, and He providentially prepares them for what He intends to use them for in the life of His church. One kind of man is not any more called than the other kind of man. Where the distinction really lies is in the particular role that the man is made for and how God makes this call known to the man.

To be accurate regarding Borgman, this is precisely what he is interested in. When he says "calling," he is emphasizing how God's purpose is made known to the man himself. But why would one man's confirmation be of a revelatory nature and the other not? The answer is not found in the concept of calling; nor even by the simple designations of extraordinary and ordinary offices. The answer is found in the era in which the men themselves are living. To put it simply, apostles and prophets met with extraordinary tokens of calling because they were living in extraordinary times. They lived in times in which God was giving new revelation and making Himself known in extraordinary ways. God was giving revelation to them and through them. When the times of new revelation ceased, men were no longer confirmed in ways that included direct revelation. Is it, then, the offices that explain the difference in confirmation, or the times in which the offices exist?

It is true that the twelve men chosen by Jesus as apostles (in the restrictive sense of the word) were called in extraordinary ways. But how could they not be? They were chosen by Jesus personally. They were trained by Jesus directly. They were eyewitnesses of His resurrection (Acts 1:15–26). No servants of God (besides the apostles) have ever been chosen like this, for no servant of God ever lived during such a time! Not even Elijah or Jeremiah, or Moses, could say that they had seen the Messiah face to face when chosen for their service. In the case of prophets, when did they exist? Prophets existed at a time when God was giving direct revelation. Though the prophets were often preaching what had already been revealed, they were also instruments of God through whom He gave direct revelation (1 Pet 1:10–12). Not only were they instruments of direct revelation, but because God was confirming the new revelation, they were often the instruments of the miraculous and witnesses of the miraculous (2 Cor 12:12).

This point about the times, versus an explanation that centers solely on the offices, can be illustrated in two directions. Timothy was not an apostle in the restrictive sense of the term, nor is there any evidence that Timothy was a prophet. Yet Paul encouraged Timothy in light of an extraordinary confirmation of his spiritual gift and calling. In 1 Timothy 1:18 Paul writes, "This charge I entrust to you, Timothy, my child, in accordance with the prophecies previously made about you, that by them you may wage the good warfare." Later, in that same letter, Paul returns to the supernatural confirmation of Timothy's giftedness and calling. He says, "Do not neglect the spiritual gift within you, which was bestowed upon you through prophetic utterance with the laying on of hands by the presbytery (1 Tim 4:14)." Timothy served as an apostolic associate, but he was not one of the twelve. Timothy's role was much closer to that of the evangelist or the shepherd-teacher. In fact, he was stationed for a time in Ephesus, and found it so troubling, that he had to be exhorted to remain there (1 Tim 1:3–4). He had to guard those people in Ephesus from false teachers. He had to preach the word to them in season and out (2 Tim 4:2). Yet his calling was supernaturally confirmed.

On the other end of the spectrum is the apostle Paul. His calling needs no explanation. The Damascus road experience was clearly extraordinary. He was chosen by Christ personally, as were the eleven who remained after Judas defected. He was sovereignly prepared, when after his encounter with Christ, he spent time with the Lord in a desert school of isolation (Gal 1:15–17). The book of Acts is full of accounts that demonstrate Paul's experience with the miraculous. Yet as the biblical record moves away from the earliest days of the church, and makes its way toward the end of the apostolic era, we find Paul's experience to be much more ordinary. Paul leaves Trophimus sick at Miletus (2 Tim 4:20). He does not heal Timothy of his stomach ailment but rather counsels him to take wine as medicine (1 Tim 5:23). In other words, the man who held the more ordinary office

(Timothy) also had experience with extraordinary confirmation, and the man who held the extraordinary office (Paul), met with ordinary struggles and limitations as circumstances changed.

This distinction in emphasis—from offices to eras—may seem insignificant, but it matters. It is true that the man called to the preaching ministry today must look to the biblical record in order to discern God's calling upon his life. He will not be confirmed by prophets. He will not meet with Jesus and be directly commissioned for service. The confirmation of his calling, though not apart from personal experience, will be ordinary in many ways. But it is not because there is no calling, or because the office he will hold is ordinary. It is because, just as prophets ceased during the time between the end of the Old Testament revelation and the appearance of John the Baptist (Matt 11:13; Luke 16:16), so extraordinary evidences belong to extraordinary times. Extraordinary confirmations are given during times of new revelation, and the miracles that confirm such new revelation.

This nuance of distinction matters because there is another caution that must be added to Borgman's. It is true that men may fall prey to mysticism and fanaticism when thinking about a call to ministry. But it is just as true that men may underestimate what the ministry requires. No man desiring to be a shepherd-teacher dare enter into that work if he has not been made by God for that task, gifted by God for that task, and prepared by God for that task. He has no more right to that office than a man had a right to choose to be an apostle or a prophet. In other words, it must be feared that we are living in a day when men are viewing the pastorate and the work of preaching in exactly the way that Borgman describes it (though their mindset is different than his). They view it as something ordinary when, in truth, it is anything but ordinary. It is an extraordinary work that requires an extraordinary equipment. It is not a work a man simply decides to choose for himself, not even when he lives a life that is a good testimony. Not even when he knows the Bible well. Not even when he thinks he might desire to spend his time studying the Bible and teaching it to others. It is not a work that he can enter into by simply going to school and getting a theological degree. The man who enters the work of the shepherd-preacher must be a man called by God, and therefore sent by God. And what is more, the man must know that God called him and sent him. The ministry is difficult. Without an assurance that you have not run on your own, how impossible the ministry would be (Jer 23:21)! It was not without purpose that Paul reached back to the confirmation of Timothy's giftedness and calling to exhort him at the very time that he wanted to leave Ephesus.

This is why, if rightly understood, it is not inappropriate to refer to passages that express a prophet's sense of calling, or an apostle's sense of calling, to encourage the knowledge of a pastor's sense of calling. Jeremiah's calling (for example) has something to say about the pastor's calling. The same God who chose Jeremiah for his work, has chosen us for the purpose He has assigned to us. The same God who uniquely equipped Jeremiah to preach His Word, has uniquely gifted us for our role in ministry. The same God who sovereignly guided the steps of that prophet from the days of his youth, has sovereignly shaped our course and providentially prepared us for what we face. It is an appropriate comparison, for the difference between the men is not that one is called in a way that the other is not.[121] The difference is in what they were called to do, the time in salvation history in which they serve, and the ways in which those callings are confirmed.

CHAPTER NINE
THE CALL TO PREACH AND BROADER CONSIDERATIONS

Some have speculated that the call to preach can be distinguished from general gospel proclamation, or the general function of teaching, by the Greek words used in particular texts. The argument is that all believers are meant to preach the gospel in the sense of evangelism (εὐαγγελίζω), all elders are required to be able to instruct and to defend from the Scriptures (διδάσκω), but those who are called to preach are those who "herald" the Scriptures. The view is that those who are called to preach are especially described by the κηρύσσω word group.

There is no question that κηρύσσω is a word associated with public proclamation. The semantic range includes "to make an official announcement, announce, make known, by an official herald or one who functions as such." And, "to make public declarations, to proclaim aloud."[122] In that sense, there are texts that indicate that preaching may be understood as a larger category within which teaching takes place. All preaching involves instruction, but not all instruction includes "heralding." Paul's charge to Timothy is, perhaps, the best example (2 Tim 4:2). Timothy is told to "preach" (κηρύσσω) the word. That is the all-encompassing charge. He is then told to do it "with complete patience and teaching" (διδαχή). His preaching, then, is a proclamation that patiently instructs. Both Scripture and experience confirm that all men are not equally gifted to publicly herald the Scriptures. That recognition, however, does not equal the claim that in the way κηρύσσω is used in the New Testament we discover the reality of a call to preach.

I mentioned earlier (in a footnote) that Lloyd-Jones made an argument about the call to preach based on how Luke used word distinctions when discussing Philip in Acts 8:4–5. His argument was that the people "gossiped" the word in a general kind of evangelism (εὐαγγελίζω), but men like Philip are called as heralds (κηρύσσω). This, he said, was why different words were used to distinguish the preaching of the people from the preaching of Philip. For this argument to be valid it would need to be demonstrated that κηρύσσω is consistently used in this specialized way, or that it is especially associated with a divine call to preach. When the various word families are examined closely, the argument does not prove true.

The variation of words, such as the one Lloyd-Jones references, can be found in contexts where the same person is the proclaimer, and both words are used in a context that speaks of calling. In Luke 4:18, Jesus is presented as one who has been anointed (that would relate to a divine choice) to "proclaim good news" (εὐαγγελίζω) to the poor. "He has sent me" (calling) "to proclaim" (κηρύσσω) release to the captives, and recovery of sight to the blind, to set free those who are downtrodden..." In that passage, God's call concerning His Son's ministry is related both to εὐαγγελίζω and κηρύσσω. In addition, when κηρύσσω is examined it will be found that all sorts of people engage in the proclamation described by this word, not just those who are formally preaching.[123]

When in search of a broader biblical indication (outside of 1 Timothy 5:17 and Ephesians 4:11) of the reality of a divine call to preach the gospel, there is a better answer. There is evidence in Scripture from beginning to end that God has set apart certain men for the purpose of proclaiming His Word. There is evidence that the calling is a special one (not extended to His people in general), and that this call results in a unique spiritual stewardship and leadership in the community of God's people. When the biblical evidence for a call to preach is examined, there is a consistent theme. We find statements indicating that God calls men to preach His word, and that those men are aware of that calling. This is the pattern in both the Old and New Testaments. God chooses a man to proclaim His message, makes that choice known to the man, and the man preaches with the knowledge of that responsibility. In addition, that knowledge of God's calling is often what sustains the man in difficult seasons.

Once the objection (answered earlier) based on extraordinary offices versus ordinary offices is removed, the picture that emerges is a consistent one. This is not a claim that the extraordinary ways in which God's calling was communicated to some on the pages of Scripture are the ways in which God communicates His call today. There are extraordinary times and ordinary times. The only claim is that the basic principles related to calling remain the same. Men are appointed by God for preaching. God makes that appointment known to those men through biblical principles and personal experience. God equips those men for the way in which He has designed them to serve. The knowledge of God's calling and equipping serves to sustain those men in the difficult times they meet with as they fulfill that calling. Whether examining God's call to Moses, Isaiah, Jeremiah and others in the Old Testament, or Paul, Barnabas, Timothy and others in the New Testament, those common elements are the same.[124] This understanding will then demand a sober examination of anyone claiming to be set apart by God for a life of shepherd-teaching.

Discerning the Call to Preach

The weighty question to be considered, once it is accepted that a call to preach is something real, is how that call is discerned in ordinary times? It is important to recognize that a personal sense of calling is not enough. Both in Scripture, and in church history, we find the conviction among God's people that a call to preach cannot be rightly discerned in isolation from the church. Reflecting on Knox's call that was considered earlier, it is remembered that the entire church was involved.

The summons that ultimately comes from God is confirmed to the preacher in a variety of ways. He is a preacher by virtue of a giftedness that has been assigned to him for that task. It is a gift he can recognize but others must confirm. Paul was not only able to refer to Timothy's gift, but the confirmation of others that bore testimony to that gift (1 Tim 4:14; 2 Tim 1:6). In Paul's own case, his gift was affirmed by the church of Antioch that sent him and Barnabas on their missionary journey (Acts 13:1–3). In addition, Paul was able to appeal to the fruit of his efforts as confirmation of the legitimacy of his ministry (2 Cor 3:1–6).

The gift that has been given for a preaching ministry manifests itself in spiritual fruit. It is a gift witnessed in the life of a man and affirmed by the church as people are edified by that man's preaching. It is evident that his teaching has the effect of clarifying what the Scriptures mean. He is equipped by God for applying the truths of Scripture to the hearts of people faithfully and effectively. This gift is also manifested in the man's own desires. As MacArthur described and Scripture affirms, he has a desire to preach the Word of God (Jer 20:9; 1 Cor 9:16). He has a great love for Scripture that is in no way disassociated from his devotion as a disciple of Jesus Christ. He has been given the necessary abilities for study, for understanding, and for communicating truth. These God-given abilities must be developed and informed, but they are already present. The discovery of gifts necessary for the ministry of a pastor-teacher may take place over time and by virtue of testing, but it will indeed be a discovery, since God makes preachers.

Spurgeon wrote of God-made preachers when he said, "God certainly has not created behemoth to fly; and should leviathan have a strong desire to ascend with the lark, it would evidently be an unwise aspiration, since he is not furnished with wings. If a man be called to preach, he will be endowed with a degree of speaking ability, which he will cultivate and increase. If the gift of utterance be not there in a measure at the first, it is not likely that it will ever be developed."[125]

External Confirmation

When considering how God equips His servants to carry out the work of pastoral preaching, external confirmation is vitally connected with personal calling. This requires external confirmation of one's giftedness for the preaching ministry by qualified spiritual leaders, and a congregation that knows the man well. But there is more to it than this. There are other areas besides giftedness that must be confirmed.

The primary place where external confirmation operates (along with a recognition of gifting) is in the confirmation of the character necessary to pastoral preaching. Apparent gifts mean nothing apart from the biblical character qualifications necessary to serve as an elder. It is a tragedy that so many are willing to overlook disqualifying character flaws because a man seems, to them, to be gifted. The character required by 1 Timothy 3:1–7 and Titus 1:5–9 is non-negotiable. It is not within the scope of this work to consider those qualifications in detail. What is unmistakable, however, is that no man is right to believe that God calls him to the shepherd-teaching role without preparing him with the character necessary to that work. As John MacArthur laments, what so many seem willing to ignore, or diminish, is that the man who preaches the word is to be an example of a life that submits to that word.[126]

Bruce Ware stresses the special emphasis that Scripture places on a man's family life when he writes, "An elder...cannot be haphazard, thoughtless, or negligent about the manner in which he oversees the culture and activities of his own home. He must have a vision for his own family, leading them to grow in the knowledge of God and of the gospel that shows an intentionality and discipline that is needed if he is to be an effective spiritual leader in the church...how a father raises his children, with the thought, care, foresight, and planning necessary to lead them to a growing understanding and faith, is a clear and common indicator of the kind of man the members of a church should consider for the position of elder."[127]

A man cannot neglect family responsibilities assigned to him by God's Word in the name of pursuing a calling. The answer of God regarding a man's calling might be given through the awareness that the man's wife cannot hold up under the responsibility and scrutiny that belongs to the ministry. God's answer might be given through the reality that health issues facing the family make a life of ministry impossible. Let a man honor God first in his home life. If he is meant to preach the gospel vocationally, the Lord will change those things that restricted him. That patient obedience will benefit him in the long term.

External confirmation also includes that which is revealed through the providence of God. When God calls a man to ministry He prepares a ministry for the man. He is at work in the man's life and circumstances preparing him and providing opportunities that will grow him and confirm his calling. When a man believes he is called to preach but opportunities for training or for preaching never materialize, there is good reason to reconsider. That is not to say that a genuine calling faces no obstacles, but that God opens the doors that make for the preparation of the man whom He has ordained to be a pastor-teacher. The apostle Paul recognized that God often directs His servants through providentially arranged circumstances (Phlm 1:10–16).

Devotional Consecration

God equips his servants for preaching throughout their Christian journey. The pastoral preacher is forever a learner. He is always first and foremost a disciple of Jesus Christ. It is possible to focus so much on the shepherding ministry that a pastor forgets that he is a sheep. Just as God prepares a man through providential circumstances to enter the ministry, so He goes on developing the man. He is destined for great joys and great sorrows. He is destined to know timely support and painful betrayal. He will learn the book that he teaches not only in his study, but as he lives out what he has learned in the difficult realities of everyday life. Through sovereignly designed circumstances, a man's rough edges are sanded off, the wellspring of his own spiritual wisdom and affections are deepened, and his heart is kept tender toward God and God's people. The Lord keeps His servants near. They are able to say with the psalmist, "It is good for me that I was afflicted, that I might learn your statutes" (Psalm 119:71). If a preacher desires to be faithful in ministry let him be found fleeing from all that dishonors God (2 Tim 2:20–26).

A Reverent Conscience

The living God does not just teach his servants to trust in His greatness, but also to know their own weakness. Pride is the doorway to disaster (Prov 11:2). The Lord's work in the life of a man called to preach is a work certain to teach that man a humble heart. The result is that God's servants approach the Scriptures with trembling (Isa 66:2). They do not rush into the teaching office (Jas 3:1). They do not rush to affirm others into the teaching office (1 Tim 5:22). This God-taught reverence produces men who understand the need to watch for themselves even as they strive to be faithful stewards of the message that they have been entrusted to preach (1 Tim 4:16). They take heed to the ministry that they have received in the Lord (Col 4:17). They are on guard for themselves as well as for the flock (Acts 20:28). The ministry of preaching is nothing if it is not a matter for the pure-hearted and those who keep a clear conscience. This is an enormous emphasis in the Pastoral Epistles (1 Tim 1:5, 19; 3:9; 4:2; 2 Tim 1:3; Titus 1:15). The man-of-God's private life must be in agreement with his public preaching. When a man allows a gap to develop between the two, he is on the road to disqualification.

A Commitment to Continuance

God equips those called to serve as pastoral preachers with the holy and healthy fear of disqualification. He grants to them, and sustains in them, the desire to finish well. The faithful preacher does not want to join those whose lives are like ships wrecked and sunken at the bottom of the ocean. Instead he engages in a holy war against sin in his own life, and keeps his heart in submission to the word he has been called to declare (1 Tim 1:18–20). His life speaks of faith, not only in the gospel promises found in Christ, but the gospel warnings that call for continuing with Christ. He is a model of perseverance. He strives day-by-day in a way that demonstrates what the endurance, and constancy, of genuine faith in Christ looks like. When he says to those who eventually come behind him that they must fulfill their ministry, and that he has finished his course, they will have an example of what that means by the life he lived, and the way he preached the Word of God (2 Tim 4:1–8).

Part Three Conclusion

God makes preachers. He chose them for their work and He calls them to that work. He gives them a spiritual gift that explains why they preach to the church, and makes them effective in the ministry of shepherd-preaching. He makes that calling known to them in ways different than He did in extraordinary times, but in ways that still assure them that they have not run on their own, they have been sent. He confirms this in ways external to them, so that their assurance will not rest on their own assessments. Their calling is confirmed in the church. Those who have been given the responsibility to guide them and teach them, and those who know them best, bear witness to the giftedness and character that makes them qualified for the ministry. These God-made preachers continue under construction for a lifetime. By the same word that they preach, in the context of passionate devotion to Jesus Christ, and through a journey prepared by the hand of sovereign providence, they develop and grow. They long for nothing more than to be found faithful, and to finish better than they started. They tremble before the Word of God that is their food, their joy, and the shepherd's rod with which they care for the blood-purchased church of the Son of God.

THE METHOD FOR PASTORAL PREACHING

CHAPTER TEN

A BRIEF HISTORY OF EXPOSITORY PREACHING

As stated in chapter one, the emphasis of this book is not on some sort of innovative method. An emphasis on pastoral preaching is first and foremost about a mindset. It is not about creativity; it is about a commitment to mandates and descriptions given in Scripture regarding the work of shepherd-teachers. In fact, a commitment to pastoral preaching will mean refusing the empty promise of unscriptural innovations offered in the name of "reaching people." Innovation within the boundaries of biblically faithful ministry means considering ways in which truly biblical principles can be better implemented. It represents the operation of wisdom. Unscriptural innovation, on the other hand, manifests either ignorance of, or unbelief toward, the principles and ways for ministry found in God's Word. It represents the substitution of human reasoning in the place of biblical wisdom. That substitution can occur in the overall vision one embraces regarding ministry, or the methods embraced in the pursuit of ministry goals. In other words, unscriptural innovation can occur in the realm of ministry philosophy, ministry methodology, or both.

So what is the best preaching method when one desires to be faithful to what the Bible teaches about preaching? What is the best preaching method for pastoring people through preaching? It is my conviction that the best method for shepherding the church through preaching is expository preaching. Church history includes some fine pastoral-preachers who were not, strictly speaking, classic expositors. But the example and experience of some does not nullify the good reasons that exist for biblical exposition. In the case of some of those who would not be classified as classic expositors (Spurgeon, for example), an argument can be made that they *were* expositors in the most basic sense of what that means.

Expository Preaching Defined

Preaching is a proclamation, a declaration of the Word of God. This definition takes into account the four most prominent verbs used in the New Testament for preaching. The words are κηρύσσω, εὐαγγελίζω, μαρτυρέω, and διδάσκω. Much has been written about these words and the richness of description that they convey concerning the task of preaching.[128]

R. Albert Mohler Jr. described the multi-faceted nature of preaching when he wrote, "Preaching is communication, but not *mere* communication. It is human speech, but much more than speech. As Ian Pitt-Watson notes, preaching is not even 'a kind of speech communication that happens to be about God.' Its ground, its goal, and its glory are all located in the sovereign will of God."[129]

All preaching can be divided into two categories. There is revelatory preaching and there is explanatory preaching.[130] Revelatory preaching may be defined as that preaching that conveys direct and new revelation from God. Explanatory preaching is that preaching that returns to what has been revealed in order to understand it, explain it and apply it to those listening. Within those two categories additional genres of preaching have been suggested. Hughes Oliphant Old suggests five genres of preaching. He suggests Expository Preaching, Evangelistic Preaching, Catechetical Preaching, Festal Preaching and Prophetic Preaching.[131] He writes, "These genres are analogous to the psalm genres developed by Old Testament scholars and are defined by the different aspects of the worship experience."[132]

An important issue, demonstrated by the genres offered by Old, is the pursuit of a generally accepted definition for expository preaching. On the one hand, Old seems to define the expository sermon more in terms of its form and approach than in terms of its content. For him, expository preaching is "the systematic explanation of Scripture done on a week-by-week, or even day-by-day, basis at the regular meeting of the congregation."[133] He distinguishes this from Evangelistic, Catechetical, Festal and Prophetic preaching. Later in his book, however, referring to the preaching that characterized what Old calls "The Wisdom School", he says, "Expository preaching discussed the text, its grammar and vocabulary … preaching presented the Scriptures because the Scriptures themselves had authority."[134] In this statement, it seems that exposition is defined in terms of its content and its approach to Scripture.

It is the latter definition that best explains what expository preaching must be if it accords with Scripture. Expository preaching is preaching that relates to the proclamation of Scripture with a mandate and in a manner that agrees with the Bible proclaimed nature of Scripture. Grant Osborne describes it well when he writes, "Exposition means a Bible-based message, usually a series taking the congregation through a book like Isaiah or Romans. A topical message can be expository provided it asks, "What does the Bible say about this issue?" and then takes the congregation through what God's Word says on that issue. Walter Liefeld says that an expository message has hermeneutical integrity (faithfully reproduces the text), cohesion (a sense of the whole), movement and direction (noting the purpose or goal of a passage) and application (noting the contemporary relevance of the passage) (1984:6-7). Without each of these qualities, a sermon is not truly expository."[135]

John MacArthur makes the connection between a right understanding of the nature of Scripture and the mandate for Expository preaching. He makes the case that if we believe the Bible to be the inspired and inerrant Word of God, and completely sufficient, our preaching should reflect those convictions by consistent Bible exposition.[136]

What one searches for, then, when looking for the biblical basis of expository preaching is the kind of preaching that was done by those who were explaining what God had revealed. It is explanatory preaching that fits the description of expository preaching. Wayne McDill writes, "The word *exposition* is from the Latin, *expositio*, meaning 'a setting forth, narration, or display.' As applied to preaching, the word has come to mean the setting forth or explanation of the message of the biblical text."[137]

Expository Preaching Traced

If the previous explanations concerning expository preaching are indeed reflective of God's own desire for preaching, then we would expect to find such an approach demonstrated throughout the biblical record.

Old Testament Preachers

The biblical preachers are many and have their beginning in the Old Testament. Enoch is referred to as a prophet in the book of Jude (Jude 14-15). Noah is referred to as a herald of righteousness in 2 Peter 2:5. The first time someone is called a prophet in the Old Testament it was Abraham (Gen 20:7). But the first preacher in Scripture who had the task of delivering God's Word by reading it, explaining it and applying it, was Moses. Moses wrote down the words of God, presented God's Word to the people and led the people in commitments based upon that word (Exodus 24). The book of Deuteronomy is commonly acknowledged to be either a long sermon or a series of sermons preached by Moses.[138] David L. Larsen comments, "The book of Deuteronomy is in point of fact a series of sermons. In his superb commentary on Deuteronomy, J. Ridderbos shows how 'the reminiscences and the exhortations give the book the character of a sermon.'"[139]

In addition to the ministry of Moses revealed in the book of Deuteronomy, there are also indications that the Levitical priests had a responsibility for teaching and may have carried out a preaching ministry (Deut. 33:10). There are other clear statements throughout Scripture that the ministry of the priest was a ministry of the Word in addition to the altar (Lev. 10:8-11; Mal. 2:7; Deut. 24:8).

The pattern is that the word that God gave is now in written form, it is read to the people and the understanding of it is communicated. What Moses and the priests communicated was not the mind of Moses or the priests but the mind of God revealed in His word. The task of Moses and the priests was to communicate this clearly, faithfully and authoritatively to the people.

Other clear examples of the reading, explanation and application of God's Word would be Josiah's reforms in response to the reading of the Book of the Covenant that had been discovered in the temple (2 Kgs 23), Ezra's ministry (Ezra 7:10; Neh 8:1-8), and Daniel's study of the prophecy of Jeremiah and the subsequent interpretation of his vision of seventy weeks (Dan 9:2-27).[140] In addition to the revelatory preaching of Isaiah and Jeremiah there are statements to the effect that their ministries involved the work of instruction (Isa 30:9; Jer 32:33).

Even when the Old Testament preachers were engaged in revelatory preaching (Elijah, Elisha, Micaiah and others) there are lessons from their lives and ministries for the explanatory preacher who engages in biblical exposition. Some revelatory preachers were also led by the Holy Spirit to have their inspired prophecies written down. The Scriptures tell us that these same prophets would often consult their own prophecies in search of a greater understanding of what they had preached and written (1 Pet. 1:10-12). The very act of writing down what had been given to them by revelation indicates that they understood the distinction between what were merely their own thoughts and the Word of God that they had received.

Even as the prophets spoke in a revelatory manner they announced that what they spoke was the word of Yahweh (thus says the LORD). The exact and fearful standard by which they were to be judged (Deut. 18:20) communicates to every preacher that his task is to simply, faithfully and accurately communicate what God has said. The inspired and recorded prophesies of all the literary prophets (major and minor) testify to the faithful preachers who delivered the very words of God in the face of great opposition and unbelief. Their courage, boldness, and faithfulness instruct expository preaching in all ages.

C. Hassell Bullock, in the March 2009 *Journal of the Evangelical Theological Society*, makes the case that the wisdom literature of the Old Testament functions as an "amen" to the Torah in terms of a theological paradigm.[141] There is, in the wisdom literature, a "preaching" that is taking place as themes from Torah are reiterated, explicated, warned about and celebrated. What Bullock demonstrates is that in many places the teaching found in the wisdom literature is not just a celebration of God's law, it is a virtual exposition of it, in terms of theological themes. Bullock shows that in the wisdom literature you find (1) Wisdom's "amen" to Creator God (Prov 3:18-20; Prov 8:22-31; Job 38:4-41; Eccl). (2) Wisdom's "amen" to the Monotheistic God of Torah (YHWH, the covenant name of God, is found in the prologue, God speeches, and epilogue of Job; is found 87 times in the book of Proverbs with only 5 occurrences of the generic name). (3) Wisdom's Earmark Phrase "The Fear of the LORD/God" (Job, Eccl, and Prov). Bullock then brings his thesis to a conclusion when commenting on Proverbs 30:2-6 when he says, "And then, in words reminiscent of Moses' language in Deut. 4:2, he cautions against augmenting the words of God: "Do not add to His words lest He rebuke you, and you be found a liar" (Prov. 30:5-6). This statement sums up the general thrust of wisdom, especially as represented in Proverbs, insisting on the inadequacy of human knowledge, and the complete sufficiency of divine revelation as it is given in God's Words."[142]

The Psalms gather up previous revelation and exposit it in song. There are entire Psalms devoted to the celebration and praise of the written Word of God (Psalm 19, 119). Many Psalms tell of events recorded in the historical books of the Old Testament. David, prominent in the Psalms, is clearly referred to as a prophet and describes Messianic promise in terms expressed by God to him earlier in his life (Acts 2:30). Much like the wisdom literature, we find statements throughout the Psalms that are explaining and reiterating truths found in the Torah.[143] These men were preaching what had been previously revealed in addition to recording new revelation.

New Testament Preachers

The New Testament preachers begin with a man sent from God whose name was John (John 1:6). The Baptizer not only was a fulfillment of Scripture, he preached a simple but powerful message of repentance that we can be sure proclaimed the Old Testament. It is unlikely that the Holy Spirit would lead John's father to prophesy concerning his son and the Messiah in a way saturated with Old Testament promises only to have John make no mention of those same promises in his task of preparing the way for Messiah (Luke 1:68-80).

The Prince of Preachers, the greatest model for preaching, is our Savior, the Lord Jesus Christ. No man ever spoke like this man (John 7:46). He read from the scroll of Isaiah in his hometown synagogue of Nazareth and preached in a way that caused wonder (Luke 4:16-22). He then applied that sermon with such penetrating and exposing accuracy that it drove the unrepentant to the desire to murder Him (Luke 4:23-30). Jesus preached the Old Testament in its true sense, for here was the ultimate author of those words, now proclaiming them face to face with men. When on the road to Emmaus, after His resurrection, He explained Himself from the Old Testament in a way that caused their hearts to burn within them (Luke 24:25-32). Once and again Jesus would handle the Old Testament in a way that corrected the false religious leaders of the Jews, put away the superstitions and human traditions that had been foisted upon the poor people, and threw the spiritual blinds up so that divine light could shine into a situation (Matt. 22:23-29).

It is amazing and instructive that the one who had every right and authority to speak without reference to anything or anyone other than Him would answer with what had already been written. Indeed, when He did this He was answering with His own words.

The preaching of the apostles and their associates is plain for all to see in the book of Acts and the rest of the New Testament. Whether it is Peter proclaiming a message that employs the book of Joel on the day of Pentecost (Acts 2), Philip preaching to a Eunuch from the book of Isaiah (Acts 8), Stephen giving a tour of Israel's unbelief and unfaithfulness throughout the entire Old Testament (Acts 7), or the beloved Paul explaining the resurrection of Christ (Acts 26:22-23), it is plain to see that these men were Bible preachers. They explained the texts of Scripture. They gave the intended sense of it. They called men to response in the light of what they preached. They devoted their lives to preaching God's whole counsel (Acts 20:27). They entrusted the men they trained (like Timothy, Titus and the Ephesian elders) with the Word of God and the mandate to do the very same kind of preaching (Acts 20:32; 2 Tim 4:2). The kind of men used to turn the world upside down were men who were mighty in the Scriptures (Acts 18:24).

Examples of Biblical Preaching

Many examples of biblical preaching have already been alluded to, but there are two that are worthy to be examined here. The first is an Old Testament example. It is noteworthy in that it reminds the preacher of a most important fact. The power of preaching is explained by almighty

God and not the preacher. Jonah became a disobedient prophet. When called by God to make his way to wicked Nineveh and proclaim a message of judgment that would open the door for God's mercy, he rebelled and ran. The result was a toss overboard the ship he had boarded in hopes of making his way to Tarshish and away from God's presence (Jonah 1:3). This prophet was saturated with the knowledge of Yahweh. He knew the gracious and compassionate nature of God and specifically stated that this is why he did not want to go to Nineveh (Jonah 4:2; Exod 34:6; Num 14:18). The second chapter, which is a record of Jonah's prayer from the belly of the fish, is a collection of statements from the Psalms. When he was vomited up at the destination for his prophetic work, he was given a simple assignment. He was only to announce what God gave him to say (Jonah 3:1-3). The great city of Nineveh, full of wicked Assyrians, repented at the preaching of Jonah.

Such was the limited spiritual condition of the vessel God used that he was angry and sullen afterward and had to be taught a lesson about God's rights (Jonah 4:10-11). What Jonah did well, after discipline from Yahweh, is he proclaimed the Word of God. It was simple, it was plain, and by the power of God it was effectual. What Jonah proves is that it is the Word of God and the power of God that makes preaching effective. God transcends the vessels He uses. That is not to say that the vessel is irrelevant. Jonah was a man clearly saturated with God's Word. His knowledge of God's character demonstrated this. His prayer from the belly of the fish demonstrated this. He was clearly a man with a sound relationship with God. He was a man who dearly loved his people, and hated a cruel and wicked nation, but needed a lesson in grace.

The second example is chosen for the reason that it is so often mischaracterized. It is Paul's sermon to the Athenians in the midst of the

Areopagus (Acts 17:22). Two things have often been asserted (by some) about this sermon. Some say that this sermon represented a departure for Paul from his normal approach to preaching. They argue that this is an example of Paul's willingness to "become all things to all men" (1 Cor 9:22). They rightly note that Paul quotes some of their own poets in the course of this sermon (Acts 17:28). Walter Kaiser (who does not present Paul in the way I am describing) identifies the poets as Epimenides of Crete, Aratus of Cilicia, and Cleanthes the Stoic.[144] The second thing some have said about this sermon is that it represents a failure on the part of the apostle. He fell prey to an approach to preaching that he determined not to repeat. They tie his words to the Corinthians—about not coming to them with lofty speech or wisdom—to this sermon and imagine that Paul learned a lesson from his Athenian failure and what they believe to be meager results (1 Cor 2:1-5).[145]

But they argue wrongly when they say that Paul was trying to reach the Athenians through a display of human wisdom and eloquence. The sermon does display the kind of flexibility and illustrative material that can belong to an expository sermon, but in actuality, Paul's sermon at Athens displays all of the trademark elements of his preaching.

Paul begins the sermon with an observation. The observation itself was neutral. He simply observes that they are religious (Acts 17:22). The sermon creates a tension to be relieved and he offers the answer when he announces that he is ready to inform them concerning the unknown god acknowledged by an altar (vs.23). He then presents the true God as creator (vs.24), sovereign (vs.24), transcendent (vs.24), self-sufficient (vs.25), all-sufficient provider and sustainer (vs.25), the author and Lord of history (beginning with Adam) (vs.26), knowable (vs.26), immanent (vs.27), omnipresent (vs.27), actual (vs.29), Holy (vs.29), and non-corporeal (vs.29).

Far from the many sermons that cater to the felt needs of people in the desire to build a crowd, Paul preached a sermon on this occasion that was packed with theological depth. Built into the sermon are points derived from the biblical record. He contends that all men and nations descended from one man. He contends, as has been demonstrated, for the nature of God and the acts of God that are attributed to Him by Scripture. He argues from the very nature of man that men should know that God is not to be worshiped in the form of idols.

Paul continues the sermon with an urgent and authoritative appeal. He proclaims God's command for all people, everywhere, to repent. This, of course, means that this God must have worldwide jurisdiction and authority. He created the world, sustains the world, is involved with the world and will judge the world (vs.31). He announces that a man whom God has appointed will carry out this judgment in righteousness. This man is the one who has been raised from the dead (vs.31). He has thus proclaimed Christ, and His resurrection. He has proclaimed the preeminence of Christ, since He will judge the world. He has proclaimed the purity of Christ, since it will be a judgment of righteousness. He has proclaimed the authority of Christ, since every man will answer to Him. He has proclaimed the true humanity of Christ, since it is by a man that this is to be done. This sermon is no theological lightweight.

It is to be remembered in the case of both sermons that what we have preserved in Scripture is a summary. The essence of the sermons is unmistakable. They are obedient to declare God's Word, they convey the authority and urgency of the message, they present the truth about God's nature and character, and they flow from theological depth.

CHAPTER ELEVEN
A FINAL APPEAL FOR EXPOSITORY PREACHING

We can be thankful we live in a day when expository preaching has been a matter of emphasis. It is not difficult to find seminaries, preaching publications, training seminars, and local church pastors emphasizing the need for biblical exposition. Trumpeting the need for expository preaching and practicing it, however, are two different things. Having defined expository preaching, and having traced its history, this chapter briefly identifies principles of bible exposition and exhorts the preacher to practice those principles.

Principles of Biblical Exposition

John Broadus listed four prerequisites to effective preaching. He listed piety, natural gifts, knowledge, and skill.[146] Looking at the biblical statements that address preaching, these four prerequisites are discernable.

God's command to Timothy, via Paul, was to preach the word (2 Tim. 4:2). This means that the preacher's message is Scripture. It is not simply a message *from* Scripture, or *about* Scripture, or *based upon* scriptural principles, but is a declaration of the Word of God. The preacher is God's messenger, declaring God's message. Preaching includes several aspects. That same passage instructs Timothy that his preaching will include reproof, rebuke, exhortation, and instruction. This will certainly require knowledge, giftedness and skill. In addition, the preacher's own piety will be tested, as he is to be faithful to do this whether in season or out of season, and with all patience. The importance of piety is also stressed in passages like 1 Timothy 4:16 where Timothy is told to keep a close watch on himself and his teaching.

The text driven method of expository preaching is found not only in the acknowledgment that it is God's message the preacher is to declare, and not his own, but also in the knowledge that the Bible is God's Word. John MacArthur makes this connection when he says, "The only logical response to inerrant Scripture, then, is to preach *expositionally*. By expositionally, I mean preaching in such a way that the meaning of the Bible passage is presented *entirely* and *exactly* as it was intended by God. Expository preaching is the proclamation of the truth of God as mediated through the preacher."[147]

Richard Mayhue states the minimal elements necessary to identify preaching as expository. (1) The message finds its sole source in Scripture. (2) The message is extracted from Scripture through careful exegesis. (3) The message preparation correctly interprets Scripture in its normal sense and its context. (4) The message clearly explains the original God-intended meaning of Scripture. (5) The message applies the Scriptural meaning for today.[148]

Timothy is told to read the Scriptures publicly, to exhort and to teach (read the word, explain the word and apply the word), and to do so in a way that remembers his gift and in a way that shows he has immersed himself in these things (1 Tim 4:13-15).

Effects of Biblical Exposition

The effects of biblical exposition are experienced on many levels. The result of faithful preaching and all that prepares for it (including personal piety and prayer) will be the salvation of the preacher himself and those who hear him (1 Tim 4:16). The result of faithful preaching in the life of the church will be spiritual maturity and stability (Eph 4:11-16). In that same passage, the effects are described as the building up of Christ's body, the equipping of the saints for the work of the ministry, and likeness to Jesus Christ. From the standpoint of its effects in the world, there will be times it is powerfully received (Jonah's preaching to Nineveh), and there will be times it is mocked and ridiculed (Paul's preaching at Athens). From the standpoint of man's response to God, God will have been obeyed, His message conveyed, and His name treated as holy.

The Theological Significance of Biblical Preaching

All that one does in life makes a statement about one's beliefs concerning God. A commitment to expository preaching is theologically significant. Expository preaching declares the truth that God is, that God has made Himself known not only by natural ways but also by giving Scripture. Expository preaching declares that God worked in and through the writers of Scripture in such a way so as to produce the recording of His very words. Indeed, the command to preach the word is preceded by a statement concerning the nature of Scripture (2 Tim 3:16-17).

Expository preaching declares that preaching is a trust for which those who speak for God will have to give an account (2 Tim 4:1; Jas 3:1).

That day of accounting will be one when every man's work is examined and tested in the full view of a God who is gracious and holy, loving and just (1 Cor 3:10-15).

Expository preaching declares a belief in the sufficiency of Scripture, which is to say, a belief in God's sovereign and lone ability to save sinners and transform lives. Expository preaching is content to strive with all one's might to preach the Word of God faithfully and to leave the results in the hands of the only one who can produce results, God.

Expository preaching declares the preacher to be a recipient of mercy who does not lose heart, for he has experienced the world's only hope. That hope is a sovereign act of deliverance in and through Christ, brought to the sinner by the preaching of God's inerrant and light giving word (2 Cor. 4:1-18).

A Plan for Development

In light of these many lessons and examples concerning pastoral preaching and the kind of biblical exposition that best serves a congregation, any earnest preacher desires to improve. Improvement in preaching requires planning like anything else. As preachers we can plan for improvement and resolve to engage in some practical steps that will contribute to that desired development. The following resolution would be a good beginning place. Take a resolution like this one into your own heart for self-examination and then make adjustments as you see fit.[149]

I desire to continue to improve as a preacher. I want to learn and to aim at ongoing development in my own ministry. The reminder that expository preaching requires a bridge from the past to the contemporary audience is a good one. The reminder that expository preaching does not end short of application is often needed. I plan to aim at development through a more careful examination (with each sermon) of whether or not my sermon preparation will yield the communication, and application to my listeners, that I desire. I will examine the outline of the sermon and the main points of the sermon for whether or not they communicate authorial intent, but also whether or not they bring the author's message to the contemporary hearer. I plan to not only listen to my sermons regularly, but also watch video (if available) with the thought of improving communication skills.[150] I plan to ask my wife and family questions after each sermon to see if these goals are being met, and also ask my fellow elders for their input. I plan to go on listening to the sermons of great expositors and seeking to learn from their giftedness and skill.

Part Four Conclusion

Pastoral preaching is not an invention. Pastoral preaching is preaching with the heart, mind, and aims of a shepherd. It is how God meant for His precious word to be proclaimed to His precious flock. The best method to achieve the desires and aims of a shepherd-preacher is expository preaching. Expository preaching is the best method because it is preaching that reflects a proper knowledge of who God is, what the Word of God is, and what the people of God need most—biblical preaching. It is the very kind of preaching that is demonstrated throughout the pages of Scripture.

This is how God ordained that His people are spiritually tended. The pastors of the church take the people of God to the Bible. There they feed them, there they guide them, there they correct them, there they encourage them, and there they entrust them. "And now I commend you to God and to the word of his grace, which is able to build you up and to give you the inheritance among all those who are sanctified" (Acts 20:32).

APPENDIX
THE FRUIT OF PASTORAL PREACHING

Of all the churches that the great apostle Paul had a ministry to, none seemed to be the mixture of joy and sorrow to his heart quite like the church at Corinth. Shocking as it is, false teachers made inroads into that church in a way that, at least for a time, colored their view of this man who had been so greatly used in their lives. He was placed in the unenviable position of self-defense in the interest of their spiritual well-being, and in the interest of the reputation of the ministry entrusted to him.

In what must have been strangely enlightening to a disobedient church, the apostle put them on the stand as exhibit A in defense against their criticisms. He said in effect, "My best argument against you – is you." The God ordained nature of the apostle's ministry was confirmed by their very existence as a church. The Lord had used Paul, through the preaching of the gospel, to bring them to life in Jesus Christ. He was able to say, "For though you have countless guides in Christ, you do not have many fathers. For I became your father in Christ Jesus through the gospel (1 Cor 4:15)." In response to the idea that he needed some outside commendation or recommendation in order for his ministry to be legitimized, he said, "Are we beginning to commend ourselves again? Or do we need, as some do, letters of recommendation to you, or from you?

You yourselves are our letter of recommendation, written on our hearts, to be known and read by all (1 Cor 3:1–2)." Later, in that same letter, he said, "If to others I am not an apostle, at least I am to you, for you are the seal of my apostleship in the Lord (1 Cor 9:2)."

Throughout this book the argument has been made that expository preaching, with the mindset and aims of a shepherd, actually serves in the work of pastoral care. The argument is that preaching is ordained by God to be the work of shepherds, so that as shepherds preach, the flock of Christ is actually tended. The contention is that preaching is a shepherding work, and that in all shepherding work, preaching is applied. In this appendix some fruit is offered as evidence. Throughout years of ministry there have been, by God's grace, many confirmations of the effectual nature of pastoral preaching. What is offered here is a small, but representative, sample of how the Chief Shepherd makes use of biblical exposition to care for His people. These are personal testimonies of members at the church I have been blessed to serve through preaching. I asked for testimonies from some who have faced especially difficult trials in recent years. They tell their stories in their own words. I trust that what you have read already has made plain that all the good found in these testimonies is to the glory of God alone.

Andrew Peck: Pastoral Preaching and a Broken Marriage

Nancy and I were both professing Christians. We married in 2003 at the Baptist church where we met in Brisbane Australia. Both in our early 20s we saw our peers in the church marrying and figured it was the thing to do. The trend was to meet through church, date for a while, fall in love and then get married. It was as theologically deep as that.

The reality for us was more like this though. Meet through church, become physically and somewhat relationally attracted to each other, eventually get entangled in sensuality and then appease a guilty conscience by "doing the right thing" and get married. Not exactly the best way to begin a new life-long relationship.

About 18 months into our marriage my career as a pilot had both Nancy and I living on a remote Island. Horn Island: population 300. This sounds exotic until the reality sets in that you are a two-hour flight away from civilization, man-eaters such as 10 ft. saltwater crocodiles and sharks patrol the surrounding waters, and entertainment consists of going to one of the two local pubs to eat an overpriced steak.

During this time on Horn Island things became frosty between Nancy and me. We no longer attended a church of any kind and slowly the sanctifying influence of just being around other Christians on a regular basis began to wear off. I look back now at my Australian church life and can see that both Nancy and I were like actors in a Christian play. We knew our lines, and enjoyed being a part of the performance, but it wasn't our reality. Our true personas came out when we were alone together in isolation and not dressed in Christian costumes.

Halfway through our time on Horn Island the wheels were set in motion to move to the USA. By the time it came for us to embark on our new adventure our relationship had devolved into two people bound together that weren't even friends. It was wishful thinking on my half, at least, that our new move to the other side of the world might solve our problems, so we pressed on.

In March of 2006 we moved to the tiny little town of Darlington, South Carolina. It was a decision motivated by a sense of adventure and ability.

As a pilot, the prospects of a job with an airline were promising compared to the aviation industry in Australia. The ability to hold a Green Card based on my marital status to Nancy gave us both a hope for a new and exciting chapter in our lives.

Darlington was where Nancy's great aunt and uncle lived and they were generous enough to allow us to stay with them while we found our feet in the USA. A sweet Christian couple in their 70s, they had been married over fifty years. Darlington First Baptist Church was their regular place of worship. The Lord used them and that little church to point me, once again, to the forgiveness and new life found in Jesus.

I personally remember hearing the gospel at church in Australia and understanding I was a sinner, but I knew nothing of true repentance and faith in the finished work of Jesus Christ. Having prayed "The sinner's prayer" I thought I was a Christian but I wasn't born again.

I defined and justified myself by my occupation, my personality, and my relationship to Nancy. Theses idols were taken away from me prior to my true conversion. Five months into our USA adventure I was still unemployed, I hardly knew anybody, and a month after finding work in Houston, Nancy chose to return home without me and wanted to keep it that way.

It was through this set of circumstances, and through the many times I'd heard the gospel, that my eyes were opened to the truth that I was in a lost, hopeless, broken condition, and that a guilty judgment hung over me. I was convicted that a longtime habitual sin had me enslaved and was one of the major factors to the breakdown of my marriage, and that I needed help.

God graciously used Darlington First Baptist church to bring me to new life, and it was there that I was baptized in 2006, but it was through the expository preaching at Founders Baptist that I grew up into my salvation.

Upon moving to Houston I didn't know anyone. That didn't bother me much as I knew I'd meet new people eventually, but now, a new creation, I desired to meet Christians and to go to church. In my infancy, I had two church selection criteria: not a Catholic church and not a tongue-speaking church. Other than that I had no idea what to look for in a church.

The Lord in his gracious providence led me to Founders Baptist Church simply through me driving past it one day. I'd seen it close by another new church that I literally walked into, and then straight out of, after I saw that I'd missed the start of the service by twenty minutes. Based on that alone, I left and went across the street to Founders, whose service was just about to start. That night I heard for the first time the Bible taught in a way that I'd never heard before.

Because of my new job I could only consistently attend Founders on a Wednesday night. That in itself was a huge blessing as I was able to sit under the exposition of 1 John from start to finish. Almost ten years ago now, I still recall being like a sponge, absorbing what was taught, relating it to my recent conversion to give me a deeper understanding of the supernatural work that took place in my heart. I was born again and my new nature was being explained to me verse-by-verse, sometimes word-by-word.

My thinking towards the trial of the dissolution of my marriage was also being challenged. I came to an understanding that Nancy and I were not Christians while together. Our lives did not pass the tests that were being presented from the pulpit and I came to understand that Nancy was never going to desire God or be obedient to His commands to be reconciled unless He gave her a new heart.

One of the greatest joys I've experienced while sitting under expository preaching is to hear Scripture explained with Scripture. To see how a biblical truth is woven together even though written thousands of years apart has been a tremendous reinforcement of my surety in the infallibility of God's Word. It is such a comfort knowing that in whatever season of life I am going through God has something to say about it and if I humbly and obediently rest in whatever truth that may be, I am right in the middle of Gods will, the sweetest place to be.

A truth I can attest to is the sufficiency of Christ. The greatest struggle I have had since coming to faith in Christ is the thought that my relationship to Christ is enough to be completely satisfied in this world. Time and time again, through the faithful preaching of the Word, I have been ministered to in a way that points me to Jesus and the abundant blessings found in a right relationship with him.

Satanic lies and fleshy desires that attack and seek to devour me have been crushed repeatedly through pastoral exhortation from the Word of God. A call to repentance and obedience, a loving word of encouragement, a refocusing on Christ, have all been the result of a faithful exposition boldly proclaimed and applied to my life through the ministering Holy Spirit.

Being a member of a church whose members sit under expositional preaching has also been an immense blessing. I have been ministered to many times by brothers and sisters in Christ who are well taught and have counselled me from Scripture. They have been fed on solid food through their exposure to expositional preaching, and have often wisely guided and counselled me in the midst of trials.

As I have now moved back to Australia, I look back with such thankfulness and affection towards the faithfulness of my pastor's expository preaching. I joined Founders Baptist Church a spiritual babe in Christ, not having a clue as to who I was post conversion. I was taught well and daily I try to behold and live in the light of those truths, fighting the good fight of faith, yet still stumbling in many ways.

I can truly testify that the rod and the staff of a faithful expositor when used lovingly are the sweetest tools on earth, and am blessed beyond measure that the shepherding I've received will continue to guide me into eternity.

Joe Patino: Pastoral Preaching and a Sick Child

My family has sat under Pastor Caldwell's teaching for nearly fifteen years. The benefits of sitting under expositional teaching for that length of time are countless. To say that we have grown in our walk with the Lord and increased our depth of understanding of biblical doctrine is an understatement. To point out an example of this, I would have to mention probably the most difficult thing we have ever gone through as a family.

Our youngest daughter was a picture of health and happiness until she was 9 years of age. We, as a family, had never gone through a truly trying time up until this point. All of that was turned around abruptly when one morning out of the blue, she had a grand mal seizure in front of my wife and me. We had no idea what was happening. We were filled with fear. One thing that I believe took Kim and me by surprise was the lack of panic and the overwhelming knowledge that, there is a sovereign God in complete control of this situation. There was great peace and comfort in that knowledge, and I attribute that to the sound doctrine we had been taught all this time.

Things for my daughter continued to get more complicated and within a year of her being diagnosed with epilepsy, we discovered that she had an extremely rare form of cancer that causes tumors to grow out of her carotid arteries. This was even more devastating than her epilepsy diagnosis as this would involve extremely complicated surgeries and would be something we would deal with the rest of Maddie's life. Again, we relied on the foundation of truth that we had sealed in our hearts and minds over the years to get us through these things.

I have known other Christian families that I would say have not sat under the same teaching that we have, that have gone through various trials that sadly resulted in a much different outcome for their families. I believe with every ounce of my being, had we not had such a solid foundation we would have had a far more difficult time dealing with all that we have dealt with. We count sitting under Pastor Caldwell's teaching as one of the great blessings for our family. Thankfully, we have three children that love the Lord and are growing in faith. We have a marriage that grows stronger by the day. And best of all, my daughter is doing amazingly well now and should live a long, happy life. Lord willing!

Liz Mauch: Pastoral Preaching and Light in a Confused Place

Dear Pastor Richard, the book I am currently reading, *The Journey*, by Adam Hamilton, in preparation for Christmas, ends the first chapter with the following prayer: "Lord, thank you for the people through whom you have spoken to me. Help me to pay attention and listen for your voice through those you send. Speak Lord: your servant is listening."

The Lord has truly and profoundly used you to teach, reprove, correct, and train me in righteousness. Often, it is precept upon precept, line upon line. Then you preach a sermon that is a capstone and an entire block of teaching is more fully understood. An example was when you preached about Christ's death being of inestimable value, and capable of saving all to the uttermost, but being divinely applied to those whom God foreknew. That was the missing link for me to more fully understand and appreciate the doctrines of grace.

Other times you've explained a passage of Scripture that I never understood. An example of such a passage is the three that testify in 1 John: The Spirit, the water, and the blood. It made perfect sense when you explained that the water was Christ's baptism, the blood was Christ's death, and they were the bookends of Christ's earthly ministry.

Last night when you used your own struggles with prayers that were not answered the way you wanted and how you handled it, really encouraged me, especially in my struggle to come to terms with the death of my dad of whom I had no assurance of salvation. The Lord has used you greatly in my life and the life of my family. Thank you!

Amber Ramirez: Pastoral Preaching and Light in a Dark Place

Note: Amber is my daughter. She is married to our youth pastor, Nathan Ramirez. She has been diagnosed with refractory celiac. It is the most difficult variety of the disease to treat. It also contributes to a great battle with depression. She has suffered from seizures, off and on, for the past year. She has two little girls, both under the age of four. It has been the most difficult year of her life. She has not been able to eat normally for months now. She uses that analogy to speak of the ministry of Scripture, reflecting on Proverbs 30:8. It is my hope that this provides context for her testimony.

Preaching is the bread and wine of the gifts to the church of God. It is sweet to the soul, rich with depth, but also at the same time easy to digest. It is essential to maturity in the life of the believer. If too long without it, it leaves one in a spiritual state of starving. It is one of God's finest and brightest gifts to His children, and a lighthouse that leads his flock to the gates of splendor.

Growing up in a pastor's home, and also being a pastor's wife, one might think I would be the least qualified to testify to the value of sound, gifted, expositional preaching. My opinion might be partial, and non-objective, wanting to glorify the vocation simply because the two most important men I love function in that office. I would argue, rather, that I am one who has a unique perspective to offer. Jesus said in Luke 4:24, "Truly, I say to you, no prophet is acceptable in his hometown." Sometimes the people we tune out the most, and are quickest to write off, are those we are most familiar with.

There have been times that the Word of God has been shared with me from my father or my husband and my heart shuts out what they have to say, because I don't think that they see things clearly, or understand me well. Only later to have them preach from the pulpit the very same message and have my heart opened up as if the Holy Spirit were audibly directing the course of the message to me. Something magical takes place when a gifted shepherd carefully exposes the Word of God for what it is. I have walked through dark bouts of deep despair and depression. Times when I did not want to live one more moment. I've prayed through those times, read God's Word, talked to other believers, and at times it was not enough. The only light that has consistently shined forth in those times has been the hearing of the Word of God preached. It is a God designated way for the life of a believer to be refined and taught. It is like the most beloved star of Earendil that was handed to Frodo from the elves when He was about to embark upon the darkest part of His journey in *The Fellowship of the Ring*. The star was described as light in dark places when all other lights go out. I can testify that hearing the Word of God preached excellently has been my Earendil. It has been my light when all other lights go out.

But it cannot be just any kind of preaching. As I have said, it must be excellent, it must be careful, and it must reflect an ability that God gives. Maturity, growth, edification, and refinement can only occur through carefully prepared feasts that are fit for the souls of the Lord's people. It must be Holy Spirit led, and taught by a humble servant who is in tune with the needs of His flock.

The church is made up of the children of God. Children do not always know the food that is needful for them (Proverbs 30:8). It takes a holy and skilled pastor to faithfully exposit the Word of God to fit the needs of His congregation, and give them their proper nutrition. If a child was left to his own, he would always choose the sweet stuff. Give me the easily digestible, sweet milk that will make me feel good immediately and leave me running on a sugar high. Problem is, if that child is continually fed on that diet he will grow sluggish, fat, lazy, and his overall health would eventually deteriorate. His body would not be receiving the essential building blocks of meatier substances that are important for his development. He would never choose the strange looking vegetables, because they look intimidating and the taste is sometimes hard to get used to. Little does he know that foods like these are vital to his survival. The faithful, loving parent must give their child not just want he wants but what he needs most.

In a similar way, we as God's children don't always have the right discernment of the food that is most needful for us. At times when I'm feeling down, I want to be filled on everything that is light in the Word of

God. It gives me an immediate sense of good. But that is not always what I need. If I continually feed on that, I neglect to see the festering self-sin that has taken deep root in my soul and must be piercingly removed through the ministry of God's Word. Sound, gifted preaching, presents the child with the food they need most. The faithful shepherd knows when his congregation needs to sift through the vegetables of hard to understand doctrine in order to make them stronger in their faith. He knows when his congregation is suffering and needs a soothing warm meal that is easily understood and digested. And he also knows when he needs to present a harsh warning they may not like the taste of, in order to get their health back on track.

Preaching has been soul filling for me at a time in my life when I have been physically starving. It has been my feasting table that I have been able to approach when I am physically deprived, only to open up my mouth wide spiritually and have it filled to the brim. And just when the preacher opens to a text that I think I don't need, the Holy Spirit shows me how desperately I do need it. We are easily distracted forgetful children and our heavenly father knows this. He is gentle and patient in dealing with us, and He sovereignly ordained a means to allow us to hear his voice on a routine basis, even though we wait to see Him face to face. I will forever praise the Lord for the marvelous bread and wine of the preaching of the Word of God.

Joe Jones: Pastoral Preaching and Stability at All Times

My name is Joe Jones. I am 34 years of age, married, and have five children. I am personally in favor of expository preaching because I am convinced both scripturally and practically that it is the best approach for preaching. Personal experience also tells me that expository preaching, especially when conducted consistently and over time, is not only a good means but the best means for pastoral work. This is true not in spite of but especially *amidst* the most difficult times a believer experiences. I would like to provide seven reasons for this conviction, followed by a summary of the way expository preaching has ministered to my family.

First, expository preaching meets our need for right thinking and right action in life's every stage and circumstance. Every believer will experience a myriad of circumstances in life, spanning the spectrum from heart-break, sorrow and grief, to joy inexpressible. No matter where on this spectrum a believer lands at any given point in his life, it is possible to live obediently and joyfully. The questions that face the believer are, "What is the will of God here?" "How do I know the righteous course of action?" "How do I know what is good and acceptable and perfect before the face of God?" Because we reside in sinful bodies on account of the fall, if we are to answer these questions well and act accordingly, we must be transformed by the renewal of our minds. This renewal then results in our capacity to answer those questions. And regardless of life's circumstances, we cannot do better than the good, the acceptable, and the perfect will of God (Rom. 12:1-2).

Second, expository preaching meets our need for spiritual rest. Many a Christian has experienced the need for rest amidst a trial. God, in His goodness, has provided us a means by which we might know that rest. As the good news is delivered, and as God's people receive His Word by faith, they thereby enter the rest of God, "For we who have believed enter that rest" (Heb. 4:3). Christ Himself also says, "All things have been handed over to me by my Father, and no one knows the Son except the Father, and no one knows the Father except the Son and anyone to whom the Son chooses to reveal him. Come to me, all who labor and are heavy laden, and I will give you rest. *Take my yoke upon you, and learn from me, for I am gentle and lowly in heart, and you will find rest for your souls. For my yoke is easy, and my burden is light*" (Matt. 10:27-30, emphasis added).

In the passage from Hebrews chapter 4, it is plain to see that it is by the faithful reception of the Word of God that His rest is realized. In the passage from Matthew chapter 10, those who know the Son are those to whom the Son reveals Himself. In either case, the Word must be faithfully preached in order for the promise to be realized. "How then will they call on him in whom they have not believed? And how are they to believe in him of whom they have never heard? And how are they to hear without someone preaching?" (Rom. 10:14).

Third, expository preaching meets our need for eternal perspective. It is not short-sighted, and it does not settle for mere earthly "happiness." I greatly fear that many well-intentioned attempts at pastoral work lose sight of the fact that we are citizens of heaven, and that our hearts must necessarily be weaned from this world. While we do not go out in search of trials, the ones the Lord is pleased for us to endure are a necessary part of our sanctification. They cause us to set our eyes upon Christ and upon the promise that awaits us, knowing that this life is but a vapor, and further, that we are being made for a heavenly citizenship. We know that.

According to his great mercy, he has caused us to be born again to a living hopethrough the resurrection of Jesus Christ from the dead, toan inheritance that is imperishable, undefiled, and unfading, kept in heaven for you, who by God's power are being guarded through faith for a salvation ready to be revealed in the last time. In this you rejoice, though now for a little while, if necessary, you have been grieved by various trials, so that the tested genuineness of your faith—more precious than gold that perishes though it is tested by fire—may be found to result in praise and glory and honor at the revelation of Jesus Christ (I Pet. 1:3-7).

Fourth, expository preaching meets our need to entrust our well-being to God. This is a need for every human heart. If we trust the Word of God, taught by a man called by God, to shepherd hearts and minds, we do not run the risk of entrusting our well-being to misinformed (even if well-intentioned) earthly wisdom—including that of our own devices. God, in His mercy, has been pleased to convey to us that it is what *He* says I am that makes me who I am, and it is what *He* says is best for me that truly is best for me. Further, this is best conveyed through expository preaching, where the whole counsel of God's Word informs the whole man.

Fifth, expository preaching meets our need for change at the level of the heart. Related to the first point above, it is only inside-out change as a result of conversion and sanctification that is genuine. For any walk of life, the Lord is pleased for me to endure, no matter how trying, what I need is not a change of circumstance. No, what I need is a change of heart in the midst of my circumstances that allows me not merely to cope, but to actually be thankful. An example of this kind of thinking can be found in a case in Acts where some of Christ's apostles are arrested, beaten, and eventually set free: "Then they left the presence of the council, *rejoicing that they were counted worthy to suffer dishonor for the name.* And every day, in the temple and from house to house, they did not cease teaching and preaching that the Christ is Jesus" (5:41-42, emphasis added). We can also say confidently that the apostle Paul knows what it is to have his heart contented amidst various circumstances: "I have learned in whatever situation I am to be content. I know how to be brought low, and I know how to abound. In any and every circumstance, I have learned the secret of facing plenty and hunger, abundance and need. I can do all things through him who strengthens me" (Phil 4:11-13). And yet Paul's charge in his pastoral letters is always to preach the living, effectual Word of God. The man who is truly circumcised of heart, not merely content but even *thankful* for his trials, is a servant of God who is also prepared, from the heart, for whatever this life may hold.

Sixth, expository preaching meets our need for confidence in the sufficiency of Scripture. In fact, expository preaching is the logical, practical outworking of a belief in the sufficiency of Scripture. Every reason I have given for my belief in the capacity of expository preaching for pastoral work is dependent upon this foundational conviction. The exposition of God's Word, book-by-book, chapter-by-chapter, verse-by-verse, and so on, gradually and eventually produces a man who knows the Word of God well and in context. In fact, the longer my family and I sit under the faithful exposition of the work, the more the benefits of that kind of teaching continue to manifest themselves. It is a form of preaching that trusts in the whole council of God's Word to equip the saints. It is a form of preaching that lends to the Word the intrinsic authority it is due. We live in a society that cannot bear the notion that external authority is *a* path, let alone *the* path to human freedom, flourishing, and spiritual health. This notion has unfortunately affected the Church to the extent that baptized psychology often persists where the Word of God ought to reign.

Seventh, expository preaching meets our need for the whole counsel of God to be taught in order to prepare the whole man. 2 Tim. 3:16-17 says that, "All Scripture is breathed out by God and profitable for teaching, for reproof, for correction, and for training in righteousness, that the man of God may be complete, equipped for every good work." Expository preaching betrays a full-fledged belief in that promise. The question every Christian must face is whether he truly believes that the Scriptures are sufficient to teach, to reprove, to correct, and to train in righteous-ness, in order that the Christian might be complete and equipped for every good work. If so, then consistent exposition of God's Word over time is unmatched in terms of Pastoral tools for the care of God's people. Hebrews 13:17 clearly gives authority to the leaders of God's people for watch-care over human souls, and the task they are given, above all else, is to preach the whole counsel of the Word of God.

I cannot recall when I was saved. I truly do not ever remember a time in my life where I did not believe the gospel wholeheartedly. Having been saved at a young age, and having grown up in a Christian home, and having grown up in church, I can say with confidence that the Lord has used con-sistent exposition of the Word more powerfully than any other pastoral tool in my own life and in the life of my family. I had a far better understanding of Scripture after only months of faithful exposition that in a lifetime prior of topical preaching and baptized psychology, and I am the better for it.

When I am doing well (or perhaps it is better to say when I have *convinced* myself that I am doing well), the exposition of His Word has shown me where growth yet needs to take place. When trials come (and come they have), our family is equipped to deal with them. My younger brother lost his wife and unborn child to cancer fourteen months ago at the time of this writing. The two years she spent battling prior to her death were the most difficult thing we have ever endured. Not far behind is the adoption of two of our boys, rescued from an abusive and neglectful environment, that saw us battling in court for a period of two-and-a-half years for conserva-torship. All the while, we dealt with the physical, emotional, and spiritual trauma that resulted from what they had endured. We cleaned up fecal matter every day, sometimes more than once per day, from a six-year-old boy with no bathroom skills. We dealt with severe behavioral problems, including anger and aggression. We worked hard to make up for lost time academically for two boys who had never darkened the door of a school. All of these things were (and to some extent still are) a burden on those boys, on my wife and myself, and on our biological children. Even today my wife's brother sits in a hospital bed on life support as two sides of the family are opposed to one another and embroiled in a legal battle over whether he should be moved to hospice in the face of his imminent death.

While unique, I know that our struggles are not out of the ordinary. We live in a cursed, sin-sick world that groans in anticipation of its being set free from bondage and corruption. I also know that that the sufferings of this present time are not worth comparing with the glory that is to be revealed to us. In the meantime, we sojourn here on this earth, where the Lord will test us, try us, and grow us. From the bottom of my heart, I could not be more thankful for the ways in which the Lord has met the needs of my family by meeting our need for sanctification—for right thinking and right action, by meeting our need for spiritual rest in the midst of our circumstances, by giving us eternal perspective in a temporal world, by helping us to entrust our well-being to the One who knows what is best for us, by granting us contentment of heart in the face of trials, by giving us confidence in the capacity of His Word to equip us, and by delivering to us, via faithful exposition, the whole counsel of His Word in order that we might be complete and equipped for every good work.

END NOTES

INTRODUCTION

[1] Samuel Volbeda, *The Pastoral Genius of Preaching* (Grand Rapids: Zondervan Publishing, 1960), 5.

[2] Volbeda's book is conceptually helpful. It is, however, a lite offering. After the preface and introduction, the work consists of 64 pages. In addition, Volbeda's sharp division between God's use of intermediaries (preachers of the word) in the work of regeneration, and His use of the same in sanctification, does not accord with Scripture (see chapter 4). The theme of the book, however, is worthy of further thought and research.

[3] Ibid., 29.

[4] Charles Jefferson, *The Minister as Shepherd* (Fort Washington, PA: CLC Publications, 2006), 52–53.

[5] Jefferson's work lays special emphasis on the shepherding motif. His book consists of a series of lectures delivered in the year 1912.

[6] Jason Meyer, *Preaching: A Biblical Theology*, (Wheaton, IL: Crossway Books, 2013), 11-12.

[7] John Stott, *The Preacher's Portrait: Some New Testament Word Studies* (Grand Rapids: Eerdmans Publishing, 1961), 23.

PART ONE

[8] One example would be Meyer's work on preaching. It is a wonderful resource but illustrates the point. In a book of 368 pages the subject index makes reference to shepherding once, on page 258. That particular reference reveals a single statement about the goal of preaching. It is an entire theology of preaching that barely interacts with the shepherding motif. See Meyer, *Preaching*, 258.

[9] Each of these titles for Christ could be unpacked exegetically and from a biblical-theological perspective. The only reason for listing them is to demonstrate the centrality of Christ's own person and character for all that the church is to be and to become. That includes the work of preaching.

[10] Resources that do an outstanding job of tracing the shepherd theme throughout the Scriptures are Timothy S. Laniak, *Shepherds After My Own Heart* (Downers Grove, IL: InterVarsity Press, 2006), and Kenneth E. Bailey, *The Good Shepherd* (Downers Grove, IL: InterVarsity Press, 2014).

[11] Unless noted otherwise, all Bible quotes are taken from the English Standard Version (Wheaton: Standard Bible Society, 2001).

[12] William Arndt, Frederick W. Danker, and Walter Bauer, A *Greek-English Lexicon of the New Testament and Other Early Christian Literature*, 3rd ed. (Chicago: University of Chicago Press, 2000), 181.

[13] Robert H. Mounce, "John," in *The Expositor's Bible Commentary: Luke-Acts (Revised Edition)*, ed. Tremper Longman III and David E. Garland, vol. 10 (Grand Rapids, MI: Zondervan Publishing, 2007), 658–659.

[14] John Calvin, *John*, Crossway Classic Commentaries (Wheaton, IL: Crossway Books, 1994), John 21:15.

[15] BDAG, 233.

[16] BDAG, 619–620.

[17] Some would not agree that the terms pastor and elder are used of the same men. The biblical use of these terms is taken up later, in the chapter entitled "The Stability for Pastoral Preaching."

[18] I am aware that the stewardship metaphor is distinct from that of shepherding. The same men who serve as shepherds, however, are the stewards of God's Word. It is also true that when one remembers that the pastor's shepherding work has been assigned by the chief shepherd, then shepherding is a stewardship as well.

[19] Stott, *The Preacher's Portrait*, 22.

[20] While priests and kings did not always preach, in the Israelite theocracy their shepherding responsibility always had a relationship to the Word of God. It is also true that priests had a teaching role among the people (Lev 10:8–11; Deut 33:10), and both David and Solomon made significant contributions in the form of instruction.

[21] See Craig A. Evans, Word and Glory: On the Exegetical and Theological Background of John's Prologue, vol. 89, Journal for the Study of the New Testament Supplement Series (Sheffield, England: Sheffield Academic Press, 1993), 29–31.

[22] Matthew Montonini, "Shepherd," ed. John D. Barry et al., *The Lexham Bible Dictionary* (Bellingham, WA: Lexham Press, 2012, 2013, 2014, 2015).

[23] Laniak, *Shepherds after my own Heart*, 58–72.

[24] The Old Testament condemns false shepherds in passages like Isaiah 56:9–12; Jeremiah 10:21; 12:10; 22:22; 23:1–2; 25:34–37; 50:6–7; Ezekiel 34; Zechariah 10:1–3. The promise of true shepherds is found in passages like Jeremiah 3:15; 23:4, and of course there is the promise of Christ as shepherd in passages like Ezekiel 34:23–24; Isaiah 40:11; Jeremiah 23:5.

[25] Prime and Begg, *On Being a Pastor*, 143.

PART TWO

[26] BDAG, 150.

[27] MacArthur Jr., *Pastoral Ministry*, 74.

[28] Stott, *The Preacher's Portrait*, 17.

[29] Ibid., 17.

[30] Ibid., 18.

[31] Ibid., 27.

[32] Ibid., 28–30.

[33] Fred B. Craddock, *As One Without Authority*, 4th ed. (St. Louis, MO: Chalice Press, 2001), 11.

[34] Ibid., 58.

[35] Ibid., 58–59.

[36] C. H. Spurgeon, *Lectures to My Students: A Selection from Addresses Delivered to the Students of the Pastors' College, Metropolitan Tabernacle.*, vol. 1 (London: Passmore and Alabaster, 1875), 2.

[37] BDAG, 362.

[38] Thomas D. Lea and Hayne P. Griffin, *1, 2 Timothy, Titus*, vol. 34, The New American Commentary (Nashville: Broadman & Holman Publishers, 1992), 141.

[39] Daniel B. Wallace, "Crisis of the Word: A Message to Pastors and Would-Be Pastors (2 Timothy 2:15)," *Conservative Theological Journal Volume 11*, no. 2 (1997): 108.

[40] A. Duane Litfin, "1 Timothy," in *The Bible Knowledge Commentary: An Exposition of The Scriptures*, ed. J. F. Walvoord and R. B. Zuck, vol. 2 (Wheaton, IL: Victor Books, 1985), 733.

[41] John Piper, *The Supremacy of God in Preaching*, Rev. ed. (Grand Rapids, MI: Baker Books, 2004), 10.

[42] Peter Thomas O'Brien, *The Letter to the Ephesians*, The Pillar New

Testament Commentary (Grand Rapids, MI: W.B. Eerdmans Publishing Co., 1999), 267.

[43] Jude 24–25; Rom 11:36; 16:25–27; Eph 3:20–21; 1 Pet 4:11; 5:11; 2 Pet 3:18; Gal 1:5; Phil 4:20; 1 Tim 1:17; 6:15–16; 2 Tim 4:18; Heb 13:20–21; Rev 1:5–6; 4:11; 5:13; 7:12.

[44] "While there is some scholarly disagreement regarding the literary genre of Hebrews, most evangelical scholars agree that Hebrews is sermonic in nature. For example, William Lane writes: 'Hebrews is a sermon rooted in actual life. It is addressed to a local gathering of men and women'. Similarly, R. T. France writes: 'There is, however, one book of the New Testament which seems to offer a closer analogy to modern expository preaching than the rest; that is, the Letter to the Hebrews.' In addition to scholarly opinion, we also have the author's own testimony regarding the nature of his correspondence. For instance, in Hebrews 13:22 the author refers to his letter as a 'word of exhortation' (λόγου τῆς παρακλήσεως). Evidence that this phrase refers to a sermon is the fact that a similar phrase (λόγος παρακλήσεως) is used by Paul to describe his sermon at the Synagogue in Pisidian Antioch (Acts 13:15). This epistle, therefore, is really an inspired sermon." (Anthony T. Selvaggio, "Preaching Advice from the 'Sermon' to the Hebrews," *Themelios: Volume 32, No. 2, January 2006* (2006): 33–34.)

[45] Ps 2:7; 2 Sam 7:14; Deut 32:43; Ps 104:4; Ps 45:6–7; Ps 102:25–27; Ps 110:1

[46] Other examples of pastoral sensitivity to specific needs would be Paul's counsel regarding marriage in 1 Cor 7 and his comfort to the Thessalonians regarding the resurrection in 1 Thess 4.

[47] George W. Knight, *The Pastoral Epistles: A Commentary on the Greek Text*, New International Greek Testament Commentary (Grand Rapids,

MI: Carlisle, England: W.B. Eerdmans; Paternoster Press, 1992), 412.

[48] Wallace, "Crisis of the Word," 113.

[49] Scott M. Manetsch, *Calvin's Company of Pastors* (New York, NY: Oxford University Press, 2013), 132.

[50] Ibid.

[51] Manetsch, *Calvin's Company*, 133.

[52] John M. Frame, *The Academic Captivity of Theology* (Lakeland, FL: Whitfield Media Productions, 2012), 13.

[53] Ibid., 13.

[54] Frame, *Academic Captivity*, 23.

[55] Alex Montoya, *Preaching with Passion* (Grand Rapids: Kregel Publications, 2000), 107.

[56] Daniel Akin, "Why Preach Expositionally to See Lives Changed for the Glory of God," http://www.danielakin.com/why-preach-expositionally-to-see-lives-changed-for-the-glory-of-god/ (accessed on 9/25/2015).

PART THREE

[57] Gene L. Green, *The Letters to the Thessalonians*, PNTC (Grand Rapids, MI; Leicester, England: W.B. Eerdmans Pub.; Apollos, 2002), 128.

[58] See John F. MacArthur Jr., *Ashamed of the Gospel: When the Church Becomes like the World* (Wheaton, IL: Crossway Books, 1993).

[59] Spurgeon, *Lectures to My Students*, 29.

[60] Ibid.

[61] R. Kent Hughes, *Hebrews: An Anchor for the Soul*, vol. 1, Preaching the Word (Wheaton, IL: Crossway Books, 1993), 65–66.

[62] Spurgeon's words of preparation for his students are never out of date: "*One crushing stroke has sometimes laid the minister very low. The* brother most relied upon becomes a traitor. Judas lifts up his heel against

the man who trusted him, and the preacher's heart for the moment fails him. We are all too apt to look to an arm of flesh, and from that propensity many of our sorrows arise. Equally overwhelming is the blow when an honoured and beloved member yields to temptation, and disgraces the holy name with which he was named. Anything is better than this. This makes the preacher long for a lodge in some vast wilderness, where he may hide his head for ever, and hear no more the blasphemous jeers of the ungodly. Ten years of toil do not take so much life out of us as we lose in a few hours by Ahithophel the traitor, or Demas the apostate. Strife, also, and division, and slander, and foolish censures, have often laid holy men prostrate, and made them go 'as with a sword in their bones.' Hard words wound some delicate minds very keenly. Many of the best of ministers, from the very spirituality of their character, are exceedingly sensitive—too sensitive for such a world as this. 'A kick that scarce would move a horse would kill a sound divine.' By experience the soul is hardened to the rough blows which are inevitable in our warfare; but at first these things utterly stagger us, and send us to our homes wrapped in a horror of great darkness. The trials of a true minister are not few, and such as are caused by ungrateful professors are harder to bear than the coarsest attacks of avowed enemies. Let no man who looks for ease of mind and seeks the quietude of life enter the ministry; if he does so he will flee from it in disgust." Spurgeon, *Lectures to My Students*, 175–176.

[63] I am aware of the arguments of Brian Borgman and others that these men represent extraordinary examples not to be applied to preaching in our day. I will interact with those arguments later in this section.

[64] Jason K. Allen, "A Conversation with John MacArthur about Preaching," http://www.jasonkallen.com/2013/11/a-conversation-with-john-macarthur-about-expository-preaching/ (accessed on 11/30/2015).

[65] This assumes that the instruction accords with biblical standards such as those found in 1 Tim 2:11–15.

[66] Stetzer is the Executive Director of Lifeway Research Division. He is the Lead Fellow at the Billy Graham Center at Wheaton College. He is a visiting professor at Trinity Evangelical Divinity School and Southeastern Baptist Theological Seminary. http://www.edstetzer.com/introducing-ed/

[67] Ed Stetzer, "Is There Really a Call to Preach?" http://www.christianitytoday.com/edstetzer/2007/august/is-there-really-call-to-preach.html (accessed on 12/23/2015).

[68] Spurgeon, *Lectures to My Students*, 20.

[69] Ibid., 21.

[70] Ibid., 18–19.

[71] C. H. Spurgeon, *C. H. Spurgeon's Autobiography, Compiled from His Diary, Letters, and Records, by His Wife and His Private Secretary, 1856-1878*, vol. 3 (Cincinnati; Chicago; St. Louis: Curts & Jennings, 1899), 23.

[72] Ibid., 27–31.

[73] Ibid., 22–23.

[74] I understand their use of the word "pastor" as being similar to the way that many churches make use of the terms "pastor-teacher," or "preaching pastor," in our day.

[75] Spurgeon's view was similar to that of Calvin's. Calvin wrote, "From this passage it may be deduced that there were two kinds of presbyters, as not all presbyters were ordained to teach. The straightforward meaning of these words is that some ruled well and honorably but did not hold a teaching office. Experienced and earnest men were appointed, along with pastors, to administer discipline and act as censors in correcting morals. Ambrose complained that this office had fallen into disuse through the

carelessness, or rather through the pride of the teachers who wanted to keep both offices for themselves." (John Calvin, 1, 2 *Timothy and Titus*, Crossway Classic Commentaries (Wheaton, IL: Crossway Books, 1998), 90.)

[76] Martyn Lloyd-Jones, *Preaching and Preachers* (Grand Rapids: Zondervan, 1972), 102–03.

[77] Brian Borgman, *My Heart for Thy Cause: Albert N. Martin's Theology of Preaching* (Fearn, Great Britain: Christian Focus Publications, 2002), 33–34.

[78] Ibid., 39.

[79] Ibid., 45.

[80] Ibid.

[81] So also Spurgeon, *Lectures* vol. 1, 20.

[82] Mark Dever, *What Is a Healthy Church?*, 9Marks (Wheaton, IL: Crossway Books, 2007), 116–117.

[83] Ibid., 116.

[84] Alexander Strauch, *Biblical Eldership* (Littleton, CO: Lewis and Roth Publishers, 1995), 180.

[85] The noun pastor is found only in Ephesians 4. I understand it to refer to a gift not an office.

[86] I am referring to a division of duties based upon divine design and calling.

[87] Ryken explains the concept of double honor in the following way: "What, then, is *double* honor? Some scholars think this has to do with compensation. Teaching elders should be paid twice as much as ruling elders, or perhaps twice as much as the widows. After all, given their qualifications (1 Tim. 3:4), most of them have families to support. However, it seems unlikely that "double honor" refers only to a church's salary scale.

There is another kind of honor that may explain what Paul has in mind, for "honor" can also mean "respect." Since the office of teaching elder is sacred, ministers who do their jobs well are worthy of commensurate respect. They deserve honor as well as an honorarium; thus they are "worthy of double honor" (1 Tim. 5:17)." (Philip Graham Ryken, 1 Timothy, ed. Richard D. Phillips, Daniel M. Doriani, and Philip Graham Ryken, Reformed Expository Commentary (Phillipsburg, NJ: P&R Publishing, 2007), 223.)

[88] In 1 Timothy 5:17 it is ἐν λόγῳ καὶ διδασκαλίᾳ. Logos in conjunction with "teaching" means "preaching." See BDAG, 599. "(W. διδασκαλία) *preaching* 1 Ti 5:17."

[89] "The exact translation of λόγος depends on each context (cf. BAGD s.v. 1a β). Here it is coupled with, but distinguished from, διδασκαλία, and most modern English translations have correctly rendered it here as "preaching" in the sense of exhortation and application. That which the preaching applies and which the hearers are exhorted to heed is "teaching" (διδασκαλία), i.e., that which is taught (cf. 4:6), although the activity of teaching could also be in view (4:13, 16)." Knight, The Pastoral Epistles, 233.

[90] See T. C. Skeat, who argues that μάλιστα is often best translated as "namely," and is often cited by those who wish to adopt this viewpoint. ("'Especially the Parchments': A Note on 2 Timothy 4:13," JTS 30 [1979]: 173–77).

[91] This is their language. I would not describe my position as a two-tiered view either.

[92] Benjamin L. Merkle, 40 Questions about Elders and Deacons, 40 Questions Series (Grand Rapids, MI: Kregel Ministry, 2008), 87.

[93] Ibid., 87.

[94] See the entry on μάλιστα in BDAG, 613.

[95] Knight wrote, "μάλιστα** (NT 12x, Pl. 8x, PE 5x: Acts 20:38; 25:26;

26:3; Gal. 6:10; Phil. 4:22; 1 Tim. 4:10; 5:8, 17; Tit. 1:10; 2 Tim. 4:13; Phm. 16; 2 Pet. 2:10) has usually been rendered "especially" and regarded as in some way distinguishing that which follows it from that which goes before it. Skeat ("Especially the Parchments") argues persuasively that μάλιστα in some cases (2 Tim. 4:13; Tit. 1:10, 11; and here) should be understood as providing a further definition or identification of that which precedes it and thus renders it by such words as "that is." He cites several examples from papyrus letters that would seem to require this sense and that would in their particular cases rule out the otherwise legitimate alternate sense. If his proposal is correct here, which seems most likely, then the phrase μάλιστα πιστῶν should be rendered "that is, believers." Ibid., 203.

[96] Thomas R. Schreiner, "'Problematic Texts' for Definite Atonement in the Pastoral and General Epistles," http://www.monergism.com/theth-reshold/sdg/problematictexts.html (accessed on 11/18/2015).

[97] When I make mention of complete parity I am not denying that elders rule the church together as one body. I am making reference to something comparable to a Brethren model that would not recognize any distinct structure and division of duties among elders.

[98] κοπιῶντες is a word that speaks of toil that makes one weary. BDAG, 558.

[99] Ryken, 1 Timothy, 222.

[100] Ryken, Calvin, Lloyd-Jones, and Spurgeon, all subscribe to a two-tiered view of the office of elder. I see a single office, with each of the men culpable for the duties assigned to the office of elder, but a distinction among elders in that some are called and gifted for a ministry of procla-mation. This view does not nullify 1 Tim 3:2 and the requirement that all elders must be able to teach.

[101] While extraneous to the current discussion, such an understanding

of calling includes implications for many in American churches who believe themselves to have received a call to preach and yet do not serve as elders in their own church. Worse still are some who claim to be preachers and have a loose relationship (or none) to local church membership.

102 There are additional evidences which will be discussed later in the chapter.

103 Later in this chapter the κηρύσσω (preach) word group will be considered.

104As another example, read the account of the calling of John Knox, *The Works of John Knox*, vol. 1 (Edinburgh: J. Thin, 1854), 186-188.

105 I am personally convinced based upon the examples found in Scripture, examples from church history, and my own observations in the current culture, that it is the normal pattern for each church to have a primary messenger. See the seven messengers' angels of the seven churches in Revelation (Rev 1:20).

106 A case for the concept of "first among equals" is a subject to be considered by itself but is beyond the scope of this book.

107 I am thankful for Jerry Wragg who helped me with this clarifying language.

108 See Ware who makes this same case applied to biblical roles within the family. Bruce Ware, *Father, Son, and Holy Spirit: Relationships, Roles, and Relevance* (Wheaton, IL: Crossway Books, 2005).

109 Even the work of evangelism is on behalf of the church, since it is through evangelism that Christ forms the church.

110 With the exception of the gifts of apostle, prophet, and evangelist, which will be examined in the next section.

111 This noun is applied to Christ multiple times in the New Testament. The verb ποιμαίνω (to shepherd, lead, guide, pasture, etc.) is used multiple

times in the New Testament to describe the *work and responsibilities* of elders or overseers. But a Christ gifted man for specific leadership in the church is only described as a pastor in this verse.

[112] αὐτὸς (he) is emphatic (vs.11).

[113] I mention that they would be designed to serve as elders since I understand apostles and prophets to have been gifted men given for the foundation of the church. While that discussion (temporary gifts versus permanent ones) is somewhat pertinent to the current one, it is too involved for the scope of this work. In addition, elders served churches in their own fixed locations, whereas apostles and evangelists would have had itinerate ministries. The pastoral-teacher would have served to shepherd a local congregation and that is the work of elders.

[114] Harold W. Hoehner, *Ephesians: An Exegetical Commentary* (Grand Rapids: Baker, 2002), 538.

[115] This is an often disputed point represented by O'Brien who writes, "The *pastors* and *teachers* are linked here by a single definite article in the Greek, which suggests a close association of functions between two kinds of ministers who operate within the one congregation (cf. 2:20). Although it has often been held that the two groups are identical (i.e., 'pastors who teach'), it is more likely that the terms describe overlapping functions (cf. 1 Cor. 12:28–29 and Gal. 6:6, where 'teachers' are a distinct group). All pastors teach (since teaching is an essential part of pastoral ministry), but not all teachers are also pastors.113 The latter exercise their leadership role by feeding God's flock with his word." (O'Brien, *The Letter to the Ephesians*, 300.)

[116] MacArthur understands the teaching ministry to be something separate but still understands pastor and teacher in Ephesians 4:11 to refer to the same office. See John F. MacArthur, *Ephesians*, MNTC (Chicago:

Moody Press, 1986), 143.

117 For a contrary perspective see Andrew T. Lincoln, *Ephesians*, vol. 42, Word Biblical Commentary (Dallas: Word, Incorporated, 1990), 250.

118 Borgman, *My Heart for Thy Cause*, 33.

119 Ibid., 33–34.

120 Ibid., 34.

121 Again, this view defines calling as God's sovereign choice of a man for ministry and the appointment that He assigns to that man by saving him, gifting him, preparing him, and placing him in ministry.

122 BDAG, 543.

123 The crowds proclaim (κηρύσσω) the news of Christ healing a deaf man in Mark 7:36. The Gerasene demoniac who is delivered by Christ does this same in Mark 5:20. These are just two examples of several in the New Testament.

124 See Prime and Begg's chapter entitled *The Call and the Calling* where they make use of those who served in extraordinary ways to teach about a call to ministry today. Prime and Begg, *On Being a Pastor*, 17–34.

125 Spurgeon, *Lectures to My Students*: vol. 1, 25.

126 MacArthur Jr., *Pastoral Ministry*, 67.

127 Bruce A. Ware, Benjamin L. Merkle and Thomas R. Schreiner eds., *Shepherding God's Flock* (Grand Rapids: Kregel Ministry, 2014), 291.

PART FOUR

128 For a great example see Richard L. Mayhue, "Rediscovering Expository Preaching," in *Rediscovering Expository Preaching* (Dallas: Word Publishing, 1992), 8.

129 R. Albert Mohler Jr., "A Theology of Preaching," in *Handbook of Contemporary Preaching* (Nashville, TN: Broadman Press, 1992), 14.

[130] James F. Stitzinger, "The History of Expository Preaching," in *Rediscovering Expository Preaching* (Dallas: Word Publishing, 1992), 38.

[131] Hughes Oliphant Old, *The Reading and Preaching of The Scriptures in the Worship of the Christian Church*, vol. 1 (Grand Rapids, Mich.: W.B. Eerdmans, 1998), 8.

[132] Ibid., 8.

[133] Ibid., 9.

[134] Ibid., 93.

[135] Grant R. Osborne, *The Hermeneutical Spiral: A Comprehensive Introduction to Biblical Interpretation*, Rev. and expanded, 2nd ed. (Downers Grove, Ill.: InterVarsity Press, 2006). 29-30.

[136] John F. MacArthur Jr., *MacArthur Pastor's Library on Preaching* (Nashville, TN: Thomas Nelson Publishers, 2005), 17.

[137] Wayne McDill, *12 Essential Skills for Great Preaching*, 2nd ed. (Nashville, TN: B&H Publishing Group, 2006), 8.

[138] Old, *Reading and Preaching*, 28.

[139] David L. Larsen, *The Company of the Preachers: A History of Biblical Preaching from the Old Testament to the Modern Era*, vol. 1 (Grand Rapids, MI: Kregel Publications, 1998), 24.

[140] Stitzinger, *History*, 39.

[141] C. Hassell Bullock, "Wisdom, the "Amen" of Torah," Journal of the Evangelical Theological Society 52, no. 1 (2009), 5.

[142] Ibid., 11-17

[143] For one example: compare Ps. 24:1 with Deut. 10:14.

[144] Walter C. Kaiser, *Toward an Exegetical Theology: Biblical Exegesis for Preaching and Teaching* (Grand Rapids: Baker Book House, 1981), 228.

[145] William Mitchell Ramsay, St. *Paul the Traveler and the Roman Citizen* (London: Hodder & Stoughton, 1907), 252.

[146] John Albert Broadus, A *Treatise on the Preparation and Delivery of Sermons*. Edited by Edwin Charles Dargan. New (23d) ed., edited by Edwin Charles Dargan (New York: A. C. Armstrong and son, 1898), 8-9.

[147] MacArthur, *Library on Preaching*, 18.

[148] Mayhue, *Rediscovering*, 13.

[149] There are many practical books that address steps for development in preaching and pastoral ministry. Among some of the best are, Michael Fabarez, *Preaching that Changes Lives* (Eugene, OR: Wipf & Stock Publishers, 2002). Alex Montoya, *Preaching with Passion* (Grand Rapids: Kregel Publications, 2000). Haddon W. Robinson, *Biblical Preaching: The Development and Delivery of Expository Messages* (Grand Rapids: Baker Books, 1980). John R. W. Stott, *Between Two Worlds: The Art of Preaching in the Twentieth Century* (1982; repr., Grand Rapids: Eerdmans Publishing, 1987). Richard L. Mayhue and Robert L. Thomas eds., *The Master's Perspective on Pastoral Ministry* (Grand Rapids: Kregel Publications, 2002). Daniel L. Akin, Bill Curtis and Stephen Rummage, *Engaging Exposition* (Nashville, TN: B&H Publishing, 2011).

[150] A helpful work on rhetoric is John Carrick, *The Imperative of Preaching: A Theology of Sacred Rhetoric* (Carlisle, PA: Banner of Truth Trust, 2002).

Made in the USA
Las Vegas, NV
16 September 2021